UNDERSTANDING
CRICKET

A Guide to Playing,
Watching, and Enjoying
the Sport

Tavin D. Spicer

Table of Contents

Get A Free Book At: go.xspurts.com/free-book-offer[4]

5

1. https://Xspurts.com

2. https://Xspurts.com

3. https://Xspurts.com

4. https://go.xspurts.com/free-book-offer

5. https://xspurts.com/

Introduction

Welcome to the captivating world of cricket, where a simple bat and ball can create a symphony of excitement and intrigue. Whether you're a seasoned fan or a newcomer to the game, get ready to embark on a journey through the cricketing universe. So, grab your popcorn, put on your cricketing cap, and let's dive into the wonderful world of cricket!

Cricket, often dubbed as the "gentleman's game," is a sport that brings together skill, strategy, and a whole lot of good-natured banter. It's a game that unites nations, sparks rivalries, and captivates millions of fans around the world. From the green fields of England to the dusty pitches of India, cricket has left its mark on the global sporting landscape.

But what exactly is cricket? At its core, cricket is a bat-and-ball game played between two teams, each consisting of eleven players. The objective is to score more runs than the opposing team by hitting the ball and running between two sets of wickets placed at each end of a 22-yard long pitch.

The beauty of cricket lies in its diversity of formats. Test matches, the longest and most traditional form, span five days and test the endurance and skill of players. One-day internationals (ODIs) bring fast-paced action to the field, with each team having 50 overs to showcase their talents. And then there's the electrifying Twenty20 format, where explosive batting, cunning bowling, and acrobatic fielding combine to create a spectacle that leaves fans on the edge of their seats.

Now, let's talk about the players. Cricket heroes come in all shapes and sizes. From the flamboyant stroke-makers to the crafty spinners and the lightning-fast pacers, each player brings their unique flair to the game. And let's not forget the captains, the masterminds who strategize, inspire, and make crucial decisions on the field.

Cricket is not just about the action on the pitch; it's also about the rich history and traditions that surround the game. From the iconic Ashes series between England and Australia to the fierce rivalry between India and Pakistan, cricket has provided countless moments of joy, heartbreak, and nail-biting suspense. The sport is steeped in legends and folklore, from the heroic tales of Sir Don Bradman's batting prowess to the mesmerizing spin of Shane Warne.

But cricket isn't all serious business. It's a sport that thrives on humor and camaraderie. The witty banter between players, the amusing nicknames, and the hilarious moments on the field all add to the charm of the game. After all, who can forget the bloopers, the crazy celebrations, and the occasional wildlife invasion that keep us entertained?

As you dive deeper into the cricketing world, you'll discover a treasure trove of statistics, records, and trivia. From the highest individual scores to the most wickets taken, cricket enthusiasts have an insatiable appetite for numbers. But beyond the statistics, cricket is a game that sparks passion, ignites rivalries, and unites fans from all walks of life.

So, whether you're watching a match at a stadium, following the action on TV, or even playing a game with friends in your backyard, cricket is a sport that brings people together. It's a celebration of skill, teamwork, and the sheer joy of hitting a ball with a piece of wood.

So, sit back, relax, and get ready for an adventure through the thrilling world of cricket. From the stunning sixes to the breathtaking catches, cricket has something for everyone. So, get your cricketing gear ready and join the cricketing craze. It's time to witness the magic, the drama, and the unpredictable twists that make cricket one of the most captivating sports on the planet. Let the game begin!

What is cricket?

Cricket, the sport that has captured the hearts of millions around the world, is more than just a game—it's a way of life. So, grab your bat and put on your pads as we unravel the fascinating world of cricket!

At its core, cricket is a bat-and-ball game played between two teams on a large oval-shaped field. The objective is simple: the batting team aims to score as many runs as possible, while the fielding team tries to dismiss the batsmen and restrict the scoring. Each team takes turns batting and fielding, and the team with the highest score at the end of the game emerges victorious.

Now, let's talk about the quirky terms and peculiar jargon that make cricket even more intriguing. You'll hear terms like "googly," "yorker," and "silly point," and you might wonder if cricketers have their own secret language. Fear not! It's all part of the cricketing lexicon. A googly is a deceptive delivery by a spin bowler, a yorker is a ball that lands right at the batsman's feet, and a silly point is a fielding position just a few feet away from the batsman. It's a world of eccentricities that add a touch of humor to the game.

Cricket is known for its unique game formats. Test matches, the longest and most traditional format, span over five days, providing ample time for nail-biting drama and strategic battles. One-day internationals (ODIs) condense the action into a single day, making it a fast-paced spectacle filled with explosive batting and tight bowling. And then there's the ever-popular Twenty20 (T20), a frenetic format where boundaries and big hits reign supreme, catering to our desire for instant entertainment.

Let's not forget the cricketing heroes who have graced the field with their extraordinary skills. From the elegance of Sir Don Bradman's batting to the mesmerizing spin of Shane Warne and the lightning-fast pace of Shoaib Akhtar, cricket has been blessed with some remarkable talents. These players not only entertain us with their breathtaking shots and magical deliveries, but they also inspire generations of aspiring cricketers.

Cricket is not just about the players; it's about the fans too. The atmosphere in cricket stadiums is electric, with fans painting their faces, waving flags, and cheering their teams with unparalleled enthusiasm. The love for the game transcends boundaries, uniting people from diverse backgrounds, cultures, and nations. It's a sport that brings communities together and fosters a sense of belonging.

And let's not forget the infamous tea breaks in Test matches. It's the time when players take a break to replenish their energy levels and enjoy a cup of tea and some snacks. It's a moment of relaxation and rejuvenation, a time to reflect on the game and discuss strategies over a warm beverage. After all, cricket isn't just about the action on the field—it's about the camaraderie and the shared experiences.

Cricket has a rich history that dates back centuries, and it has given rise to numerous legendary rivalries, such as the Ashes battle between England and Australia. These rivalries add a layer of excitement and intensity to the game, captivating fans and fueling the competitive spirit.

So, whether you're a cricket aficionado or new to the sport, cricket offers a blend of skill, drama, and good-natured fun. It's a game that keeps you on the edge of your seat and makes you appreciate the beauty of teamwork, strategy, and sportsmanship.

In conclusion, cricket is more than just a game—it's a passion that has woven itself into the fabric of many cultures. It has its own language, its own rituals, and its own unique charm. So, pick up that cricket bat, immerse yourself in the joy of the game, and let cricket cast its spell on you. Remember, in cricket, anything can happen, and that's what makes it truly extraordinary!

Brief history of cricket

Cricket, a game that has captured the hearts of millions, has a history as rich and intriguing as the sport itself. So, grab your cricket bat and get ready for a journey through time as we explore the origins and evolution of this beloved game.

Cricket's roots can be traced back to the 16th century in England, where it was initially played by shepherds and farmworkers in the rural countryside. Legend has it that the game was born when a shepherd, tired of tending to his flock, used his crook to hit a stone, and thus, the rudimentary version of cricket was born. It seems like even boredom can give birth to greatness!

Over the years, cricket gained popularity and underwent various transformations. The game's early versions were informal and lacked standardized rules. It was during the 18th century that cricket began to take shape as a formal sport, with the establishment of the Marylebone Cricket Club (MCC) and the creation of the Laws of Cricket.

During the 19th century, cricket started spreading its wings beyond England. The British Empire played a significant role in introducing the game to its colonies, and cricket became a symbol of imperial influence. It quickly gained popularity in countries like India, Australia, and the West Indies, becoming an integral part of their sporting culture.

The 20th century witnessed cricket's evolution into different formats. Test cricket, the longest and most traditional form, gained prominence and became the ultimate test of skill and endurance. One-day internationals (ODIs) were introduced in the 1970s, bringing a new dimension to the game with limited overs and higher scoring rates. And finally, the fast-paced and explosive Twenty20 (T20) format emerged in the 21st century, captivating audiences with its thrilling encounters and high entertainment value.

Cricket has also witnessed some remarkable milestones and memorable moments throughout its history. From the legendary Don Bradman's astonishing batting average of 994 to the fierce rivalry between England and Australia in the Ashes series, cricket has produced numerous iconic performances that have become part of sporting folklore.

Humorously, cricket has also seen its fair share of peculiar incidents. Remember the time when a flock of seagulls disrupted play during a match in England, forcing the players to dive for cover? Or the occasion when a streaker ran across the field, evading the frantic efforts of the security guards? These instances remind us that cricket is not just about serious competition but also moments of unexpected hilarity.

In recent years, cricket has embraced technology to enhance the game and ensure fair play. The introduction of technologies like Hawk-Eye, Snickometer, and DRS (Decision Review System) has added a new dimension to decision-making and sparked heated debates among players, fans, and commentators.

Cricket has evolved from a humble pastime to a global phenomenon that unites nations, cultures, and people from all walks of life. It has transcended borders, becoming a powerful symbol of unity and a source of national pride for many countries.

As we celebrate the history of cricket, it's important to acknowledge the immense passion and dedication of the players, officials, and fans who have contributed to the sport's growth and popularity. Their love for the game has shaped cricket into the global sensation it is today.

In conclusion, the history of cricket is a tapestry woven with stories of passion, skill, and unforgettable moments. From its humble origins to its global reach, cricket has entertained and inspired generations. So, whether you're an avid fan or a casual observer, cricket's colorful history invites you to be part of its ongoing journey and to revel in the joy and excitement it brings.

Overview of the sport

Cricket, the sport that can simultaneously captivate and confuse, is a unique game that has enthralled fans around the world for centuries. So, grab your pads, dust off your cricket bat, and let's dive into an overview of this fascinating sport.

At its core, cricket is a bat-and-ball game played between two teams, each consisting of eleven players. The objective is simple: score more runs than the opposing team. But don't be fooled, cricket has a reputation for its complex rules and terminology that can leave even the most dedicated fans scratching their heads.

The game is typically played on an oval-shaped field called a cricket pitch. The pitch has a rectangular area called the wicket at each end, consisting of three wooden stumps and two bails perched on top. The batting team aims to score runs by hitting the ball with their bat and running between the wickets, while the fielding team tries to dismiss the batsmen and restrict their scoring.

Cricket is divided into different formats, each with its own set of rules and durations. Test cricket is the longest format, lasting up to five days, and is regarded as the ultimate test of a player's skills and endurance. One-day internationals (ODIs) are limited-overs matches that are completed in a single day, usually consisting of 50 overs per team. And then there's the fast-paced and action-packed Twenty20 (T20) format, where matches are completed in just a few hours.

Now, let's talk about the players. Each team has a combination of batsmen, bowlers, and fielders. Batsmen aim to score runs by hitting the ball, while bowlers attempt to dismiss the batsmen by delivering the ball with various techniques, including fast pace, spin, and swing. Fielders are strategically positioned to catch the ball, stop runs, and attempt run-outs. All players must possess a unique blend of skill, strategy, and mental fortitude to excel in this game.

Humorously, cricket is known for its unusual terminology and colorful expressions. You may hear phrases like "sticky wicket," which refers to a difficult playing condition, or "googly," a deceptive delivery by a spin bowler. And let's not forget the witty commentary and banter between players and commentators that add an extra dose of entertainment.

Cricket has produced iconic rivalries that have captivated fans for generations. The Ashes, a fierce battle between England and Australia, is one such example. This legendary contest has a rich history and is played with an intensity that only a traditional rivalry can evoke.

One of the unique aspects of cricket is the tea break, where players take a break and enjoy a cup of tea and some refreshments. It's a cherished tradition that adds a touch of elegance to the game. After all, what better way to strategize than over a cuppa?

Cricket has a global following, with countries like India, Australia, England, Pakistan, and the West Indies boasting passionate fan bases. The sport brings people together, fostering a sense of camaraderie and shared excitement. Whether you're cheering for your national team or engrossed in a local club match, cricket has a way of uniting people from all walks of life.

In conclusion, cricket is more than just a sport. It's a cultural phenomenon that has stood the test of time. From its intricate rules to its moments of sheer brilliance, cricket continues to captivate and entertain millions worldwide. So, whether you're a seasoned cricket enthusiast or a curious newcomer, embrace the humor, embrace the excitement, and join the ever-growing cricketing family.

Understanding the Basics of Cricket

Cricket, the sport that can make your head spin faster than a googly delivery, is a game that is loved and cherished by fans across the globe. If you find yourself puzzled by terms like LBW, silly point, or leg glance, fear not! Let's break down the basics of cricket in an entertaining and informative way.

At its core, cricket is a bat-and-ball game played between two teams. Each team consists of eleven players, which can sometimes be confusing when you see a dozen people running around the field. It's a classic case of "one too many" players trying to sneak in for a quick game.

The objective of the game is to score runs while dismissing the opposing team. The team that scores the most runs emerges victorious. Sounds simple enough, right? Well, hold on to your hats, because cricket has more twists and turns than a Bollywood movie plot.

The game is played on an oval-shaped field called a cricket pitch. In the center of the pitch, there are three wooden stumps at each end, topped with delicate little bails that are just waiting to be knocked off. These stumps and bails serve as the wicket, and the bowlers' ultimate goal is to hit them and send them flying like a seagull stealing your sandwich at the beach.

Now, let's talk about the players. There are two main types: batsmen and bowlers. Batsmen, armed with their trusty cricket bat, stand at each end of the pitch and try to hit the ball thrown by the bowler. Their job is to score runs and protect those precious wickets like they're guarding the last slice of pizza.

On the other hand, bowlers have the tricky task of delivering the ball towards the batsmen with various techniques. Some bowls are as fast as a rocket, leaving the batsman in a state of shock, while others spin like a whirlwind, making the batsman's head spin faster than a spinning top.

Fielders play an equally crucial role. They are strategically positioned across the field, ready to pounce on any ball hit by the batsman. Their aim is to catch the ball, stop it from reaching the boundary, and attempt run-outs like a stealthy ninja catching the bad guys.

Cricket is played in different formats, each with its own set of rules and time limits. Test matches are the marathon of cricket, lasting up to five days and providing ample time for spectators to practice their patience and bring along a picnic basket. One-day internationals (ODIs) are shorter, completed within a day, and perfect for those with a shorter attention span.

And then there's the adrenaline-pumping Twenty20 (T20) format, designed for those who want their cricket served fast and furious, like a spicy street food snack that leaves you wanting more.

While cricket may seem complex, it has a way of bringing people together. The excitement of a close match, the shared joy of a boundary hit, and the despair of a dropped catch create an atmosphere that is second to none.

So, next time you find yourself watching a cricket match and feeling a bit lost, remember to keep your eye on the ball, embrace the eccentric terminology, and enjoy the camaraderie of fellow fans. After all, cricket is not just a game; it's a never-ending journey filled with drama, triumphs, and the occasional rain delay that gives you ample time to run for cover and order another round of snacks.

Cricket equipment and field

Cricket, the sport that combines athleticism with fashion, has its fair share of quirky equipment and a uniquely designed field. So, let's dive into the world of cricket gear and the unconventional playing field with a dash of humor.

First, let's talk about the cricket bat. It's not your ordinary stick; it's a masterpiece crafted from willow, lovingly shaped and polished to perfection. It's the cricketer's weapon of choice, allowing them to hit soaring sixes and graceful cover drives that make you wonder if they were born with a bat in their hands.

Now, let's move on to the wicket-keeping gear. The wicket-keeper, the unsung hero behind the stumps, is equipped with gloves that are not your average winter mittens. These gloves have padded palms to protect their hands from the fiery deliveries, ensuring they can catch the ball with the grace of a ballet dancer. And let's not forget the helmet, a must-have for wicket-keepers, because when the ball is flying towards them at lightning speed, a well-protected head is always a good idea.

Next up, we have the bowler, the master of spin and speed. They don't step onto the field empty-handed; they carry a bag of tricks known as the bowling equipment. This includes the cricket ball, which is handcrafted and meticulously stitched, ready to swing, spin, or skid across the pitch. And let's not forget about the bowling shoes, specially designed to provide the perfect grip on the pitch, ensuring the bowler doesn't go sliding like a penguin on ice.

Now, let's shift our focus to the cricket field. It's not your typical rectangular green patch; it's an oval-shaped arena with a host of intriguing features. At the center of the field lies the pitch, the sacred ground where the battle between batsman and bowler unfolds. It's like the red carpet of cricket, inviting players to showcase their skills and providing the perfect stage for drama and excitement.

The boundary, the ultimate destination for batsmen aiming to hit a six, is not marked by a simple line. It's adorned with ropes, ensuring that the ball's journey over the boundary is celebrated with a flourish, like a Bollywood star walking down the red carpet.

But what about those peculiar markings on the field? The creases, resembling mystical symbols etched into the ground, play a vital role. The popping crease, where the batsman takes his stance, is like a line of demarcation, separating him from the bowler's wrath. The return crease, a line that stretches towards the sky like a ladder to heaven, is the marker for the bowler's delivery stride.

And then there's the fielding positions, a strategic formation of players like a game of human chess. From silly point, where the fielder stands just inches away from the batsman, to long-off, where fielders wait like hungry lions hoping for a catch, each position has its own charm and importance.

Cricket, with its unique equipment and field design, is a sport that embraces its idiosyncrasies. It's a game where the bat becomes a magic wand, the pitch turns into a battleground, and the fielders become acrobats defying gravity.

So, next time you watch a cricket match, pay attention to the equipment and marvel at the intricate details of the field. Appreciate the craftsmanship behind the bat, the agility of the fielders, and the strategic placement of players.

And remember, cricket is not just a game; it's a symphony of skill, creativity, and a touch of madness. So, grab your bat, lace up your shoes, and step onto the field, because in cricket, anything can happen, from a blistering century to a spectacular catch that leaves you in awe.

Cricket rules and gameplay

Cricket, a sport that blends strategy, athleticism, and a touch of British eccentricity, is governed by a set of rules that keep the game fair and entertaining. So, grab your tea and scones as we unravel the intriguing rules and gameplay of cricket, with a sprinkle of humor.

The objective of cricket is simple: score more runs than the opposing team. But how do you do that? Well, let's start with the basics. Each team consists of 11 players, with one team batting and the other team fielding.

The batting team's objective is to score runs by hitting the ball and running between two sets of wooden stumps, called the crease, situated at each end of the pitch. The defending team, or fielding team, tries to dismiss the batsmen and prevent them from scoring runs.

Now, let's talk about the bowler, the master of ball delivery. The bowler has the task of delivering the ball to the batsman with precision and skill. They can deliver the ball in various ways, such as fast-paced deliveries, spin, or even slow, tantalizing deliveries that test the patience of the batsman.

The batsman, on the other hand, must use their bat to defend their stumps and score runs. They can hit the ball in any direction, aiming to get it past the fielders and away from their clutches. But be careful, because if the fielders catch the ball before it hits the ground, the batsman is out, and they have to walk back to the pavilion with a sheepish smile.

Speaking of getting out, there are several ways a batsman can be dismissed. The most common form of dismissal is when the ball hits the stumps and dislodges the bails, known as getting bowled. Other forms of dismissal include getting caught by a fielder, getting stumped when the wicket-keeper removes the bails while the batsman is out of the crease, or getting run out when the fielding team successfully removes the bails before the batsman reaches the crease.

But wait, there's more! Cricket also has its fair share of boundaries and sixes. When the batsman hits the ball and it crosses the boundary without touching the ground, it's called a boundary and earns the batting team four runs. And if the batsman hits the ball over the boundary without touching the ground, it's a glorious six, worth, you guessed it, six runs. It's like hitting a hole-in-one in golf, but with a bit more flair.

The game of cricket is divided into innings, with each team having a chance to bat and field. The duration of the game can vary, from one-day matches to the iconic five-day test matches, where stamina and patience are put to the ultimate test.

So, the next time you find yourself watching a cricket match, keep an eye on the bowlers, the batsmen, and the fielders as they dance to the tune of the game's rules. Marvel at the precision of the bowler's deliveries, the elegance of the batsman's strokes, and the agility of the fielders as they chase the ball like dogs chasing a squirrel.

Cricket is not just a sport; it's a theatrical performance that keeps you on the edge of your seat. So, sit back, relax, and enjoy the game, because in cricket, anything can happen, from miraculous comebacks to nail-biting finishes that leave you biting your nails in anticipation.

Scoring and terminology

Cricket, a game that perplexes outsiders with its complex scoring system and peculiar terminology, is as delightful as a mystery novel. So, grab your detective hat and let's unravel the secrets of scoring and the quirky language of cricket, with a touch of humor.

In cricket, scoring revolves around the accumulation of runs. A run is scored when the batsmen complete a run between the creases at either end of the pitch. But it's not as simple as it sounds. A single run is worth one point, while a boundary, when the ball reaches the boundary rope without touching the ground, earns the batting team four runs. And if the batsman hits the ball over the boundary without touching the ground, it's a majestic six, worth six runs. It's like winning a jackpot, but with a bat and ball.

Now, let's dive into the labyrinth of cricket terminology. First up, we have the wicket, which refers to the set of three stumps and two bails. When a bowler successfully hits the stumps and dislodges the bails, it's called a wicket. The bowler is overjoyed, while the batsman laments their misfortune.

Next, we have the fielding positions, which are named after the geographic regions on the cricket field. We have silly point, a fielder who stands very close to the batsman and hopes to catch the ball hit by the bat with lightning-fast reflexes. Then there's backward point, a fielder positioned behind the batsman on the off side, ready to pounce on any wayward shots. And let's not forget long leg, a fielder stationed in the outfield who tries to prevent the ball from crossing the boundary with their superhuman speed.

Now, let's talk about the batsman's favorite term: century. No, it's not about a hundred-year-old vampire, but rather a momentous milestone in cricket. A century is scored when a batsman reaches 100 runs individually. It's a cause for celebration, as the crowd erupts in applause, and the batsman raises their bat triumphantly, basking in the glory of their achievement.

On the other hand, there's the dreaded term: duck. No, we're not talking about a quacking bird, but rather a score of zero by a batsman. It's a moment of despair, as the batsman trudges back to the pavilion, their head held low, like a penguin without its wings.

Cricket also has its fair share of quirky terms. For instance, a googly is a deceptive delivery by a spin bowler that spins in the opposite direction of what the batsman expects. It's like a magician's trick, leaving the batsman bewildered and scratching their head in confusion. And then there's the yorker, a delivery that hits the base of the stumps, making the batsman feel like they've been hit by a speeding train. It's not pleasant, but it adds spice to the game.

So, the next time you find yourself watching a cricket match, pay attention to the scoring and the colorful language of the game. Cheer for the boundaries and sixes, gasp at the wickets, and chuckle at the amusing terminology. Cricket is not just a sport; it's a language of its own, filled with twists, turns, and a touch of whimsy.

So, sit back, relax, and enjoy the game. Embrace the joy of the run, the thrill of the wicket, and the whimsical language that sets cricket apart. Because in cricket, as in life, it's not just about the destination; it's about the journey, the moments that make you laugh, cheer, and sometimes scratch your head in bewilderment.

Playing Cricket: Batting

Playing cricket is like embarking on a thrilling adventure, and when it comes to batting, it's the batsman who takes center stage. Grab your bat and let's delve into the world of batting in cricket, with a sprinkle of humor.

The batsman's mission is to score runs, entertain the crowd, and leave the opposition scratching their heads. But it's no walk in the park. The bowlers are cunning and determined to send the batsman back to the pavilion with a sheepish grin.

To start off, let's talk about the stance. Picture a flamingo gracefully standing on one leg, that's the elegance a batsman seeks. The stance involves a firm grip on the bat, like holding onto a chocolate bar, ready to devour it with gusto. The feet are planted firmly, just like a tree rooted in the ground, providing stability and balance.

Now, as the bowler charges in like a raging bull, the batsman must anticipate their delivery. It's a battle of wits, a game of cat and mouse. The batsman's eyes are fixed on the bowler's hand, trying to decipher the secret language of their wrist movement.

As the ball hurtles towards the batsman, they must decide which shot to play. It's like choosing between a buffet of delectable treats. The straight drive, a graceful shot that sends the ball racing along the ground like a cheetah. The pull shot, where the batsman swings their bat like a mighty hammer, aiming to send the ball soaring over the boundary like a rocket.

But it's not all about power and elegance; there's also the art of placement. The batsman becomes a skilled painter, using their bat as a brush, delicately guiding the ball into the gaps between fielders. It's like creating a masterpiece on the canvas of the cricket field.

Timing is everything in cricket, just like in comedy. A perfectly timed shot feels like delivering the punchline of a joke, leaving the fielders and the crowd in stitches. It's the sweet spot, the moment when the bat connects with the ball, and it feels like hitting a bullseye in darts.

But beware! The bowlers are cunning creatures, capable of delivering tricky deliveries that can deceive even the most skilled batsman. The googly, a spinning delivery that goes against the batsman's expectations, is like a magician's trick, leaving them scratching their head in bewilderment.

And let's not forget the slips and the wicketkeeper, the cackling hyenas waiting for the batsman to make a mistake. They pounce on any edges or missed shots, hoping to snatch the ball out of thin air, like a magician catching a dove.

So, as you step onto the cricket pitch, remember to embrace the art of batting. It's a blend of elegance, power, and timing. It's about outsmarting the bowler, entertaining the crowd, and savoring the thrill of hitting boundaries.

But above all, enjoy the game. Laugh at the funny bounces, cheer for the well-timed shots, and marvel at the battle between bat and ball. Cricket is not just a sport; it's a journey filled with moments of triumph, disappointment, and a whole lot of fun.

So, grab your bat, unleash your inner artist, and let the game begin! And remember, in cricket, as in life, it's not just about winning or losing; it's about the joy of playing and the memories you create along the way.

Batting technique and stance

Batting in cricket is like performing a carefully choreographed dance on a stage set with 22 yards of lush green grass. It's a mix of technique, skill, and a touch of humor. So, grab your bat and let's explore the art of batting technique and stance in the world of cricket.

The first step is to find the perfect stance. Imagine yourself as a superhero, ready to unleash your powers. Stand tall, with your feet shoulder-width apart, and imagine you're about to save the world with your bat.

The grip on the bat is crucial, just like holding a delicate sandwich. You don't want it slipping away, nor do you want to squeeze it too tight and turn it into crumbs. Find that sweet spot of balance and control, ensuring your hands are relaxed and ready for action.

Now, let's talk about the footwork. It's like a well-choreographed dance routine, with your feet moving in sync with the bowler's delivery. Light, nimble steps allow you to adjust your position and play the shot with precision. It's as if you're dodging raindrops in a sudden downpour.

As the bowler charges in, your eyes are locked on the ball, just like a hawk spotting its prey. Focus is key, like trying to spot your favorite celebrity in a crowded room. Watch the ball like a hawk watches a juicy piece of meat, ready to pounce on any opportunity.

Timing is everything, my friend. It's like catching a train at the last second or missing it by a fraction. Wait for the ball to come to you, just like waiting for your food to be served at a fancy restaurant. It's all about patience and anticipation.

The backlift is your secret weapon. Lift the bat like a magician revealing a hidden card. It's a delicate balance between raising it too high, giving away your intentions, or keeping it too low, leaving you vulnerable. Find the Goldilocks zone, where it's just right, ready to strike.

And now, it's time for the shot selection. It's like choosing between different flavors of ice cream. The straight drive, a classic choice, sends the ball racing down the ground like a bullet. The cut shot, like slicing a piece of cake, sends the ball flying past the fielders. The lofted shot, a daring move, is like throwing caution to the wind and going for the extra scoop of ice cream.

Remember, my friend, cricket is a team sport. Communication is key. Shout "Yes!" like you've won a lottery when calling for a run, and "No!" like you've just dodged a speeding train when deciding against it. It's all about clarity and avoiding collisions on the pitch.

So, there you have it, the art of batting technique and stance in cricket. It's a blend of grace, timing, and a pinch of humor. Find your own style, unleash your inner superhero, and embrace the joy of batting.

But remember, cricket is a game of ups and downs, just like a rollercoaster ride. Enjoy the highs and learn from the lows. Laugh at the funny bounces, celebrate the well-executed shots, and savor every moment of the game.

Now, go out there, my fellow cricketer, and showcase your batting skills with style and panache. Let the opposition bowlers tremble at the sight of your impeccable technique and stance. And above all, have fun and create memories that will last a lifetime.

Types of cricket shots

Cricket, the gentlemen's game, is a canvas for players to showcase their creativity and artistry with the bat. In this lively chapter, we'll delve into the world of cricket shots, those delightful strokes that make the spectators gasp in awe and the fielders scramble in desperation.

Let's start with the classic and elegant straight drive, often described as poetry in motion. It's like sipping a cup of perfectly brewed tea, smooth and satisfying. The ball leaves the bat like a well-behaved student leaving the classroom, racing along the ground with grace and precision.

Next up is the cover drive, a shot that exudes elegance and style. It's like a swan gracefully gliding across a serene lake. The batsman leans forward, caressing the ball through the gap between fielders, leaving them in a state of bewilderment. It's a stroke that even the cricket gods would applaud.

Now, imagine a wild stallion galloping across an open field. That's the pull shot for you. The batsman rocks back on their heels, swinging the bat with authority and power. The ball rises like a startled bird, soaring over the fielders and crashing into the boundary ropes. It's a shot that announces the batsman's dominance.

But wait, there's more! The lofted shot, a daring adventure in the world of cricket. It's like a trapeze artist soaring through the air, defying gravity. The batsman takes a leap of faith, launching the ball into the sky, inviting destiny to carry it to safety or into the hands of a fielder. It's a shot that brings a mix of excitement and anxiety, for both the batsman and the spectators.

Now, let's talk about the sweep shot, a move that requires precision and courage. It's like navigating through a maze with calculated steps. The batsman bends their knees and sweeps the ball across the ground, carefully evading the fielders. It's a shot that demands skill and composure, like a tightrope walker inching their way to the other side.

And how can we forget the reverse sweep, a shot that challenges tradition and conventions? It's like writing with your non-dominant hand, a deliberate act of defiance. The batsman switches their hands on the bat handle and sweeps the ball in the opposite direction. It's a shot that leaves the bowler and fielders scratching their heads in confusion, wondering what just happened.

Lastly, we have the delicate and delightful flick shot. It's like a painter delicately brushing the canvas with vibrant colors. The batsman flicks their wrists, guiding the ball with finesse and precision. The ball whispers past the fielders, sneaking into the gaps with subtlety. It's a shot that requires a gentle touch, like playing a gentle melody on a piano.

So, my fellow cricket enthusiasts, these are just a few glimpses into the world of cricket shots. Each shot is like a brushstroke on a masterpiece, adding to the beauty and excitement of the game. Whether it's the classic drives, the daring lofted shots, or the unconventional sweeps, these strokes create the magic that keeps cricket fans on the edge of their seats.

Next time you watch a game, pay attention to the batsmen's shot selection and marvel at the variety and creativity they bring to the pitch. And if you ever find yourself playing cricket, channel your inner artist, embrace the shots with confidence, and let the ball become your canvas for cricketing brilliance.

Strategies for scoring runs

Cricket, the game of strategy and tactics, offers numerous ways to score runs and dominate the opposition. In this entertaining chapter, we'll explore some strategies that batsmen employ to accumulate runs and keep the scoreboard ticking, all while adding a dash of humor to the mix.

Firstly, let's discuss the importance of rotating the strike. This strategy is like a well-choreographed dance routine between the batsmen. It involves stealing quick singles and twos, keeping the fielders on their toes and the bowlers frustrated. It's like a game of musical chairs, with the batsmen constantly changing ends, leaving the fielders guessing and their captain scratching their head.

Another key strategy is finding the gaps in the field. It's like a treasure hunt where the batsmen search for the elusive holes in the fielding positions. They maneuver the ball expertly, threading it through the fielders as if they were weaving a delicate tapestry. It's a game of cat and mouse, with the batsmen teasing the fielders, luring them into the wrong positions, and then striking with precision.

Timing is everything in cricket, and the art of placement is crucial. It's like playing darts, aiming for the bullseye. The batsmen use the bowler's pace and the fielding positions to their advantage, guiding the ball with finesse to the areas where the fielders are not. It's a skill that requires precision and control, like hitting a moving target with a rubber band.

Now, let's not forget the power game. Sometimes, brute force is the answer. It's like a battering ram smashing through the castle gates. The batsman uses raw power to send the ball soaring over the boundary ropes, leaving the fielders and the crowd in awe. It's a strategy that requires strength and a fearless mindset, like facing a charging rhinoceros.

A clever strategy is to target the weaker bowlers in the opposition. It's like picking the ripest fruit from the tree. The batsmen identify the bowlers who struggle with accuracy or pace and take advantage of their shortcomings. It's a psychological game, where the batsman preys on the bowler's insecurities, like a cunning fox outsmarting its prey.

Adapting to different game situations is a crucial aspect of scoring runs. It's like being a chameleon, blending into the environment. The batsman reads the game, assesses the field placements, and adjusts their stroke play accordingly. They switch gears effortlessly, shifting from defense to attack, like a race car driver maneuvering through different terrains.

Lastly, let's not forget the value of patience and discipline. It's like a game of chess, where the batsman carefully plans their moves. They resist the temptation to play rash shots and wait for the right moment to strike. It's a mental battle, where the batsman stays focused and determined, like a monk meditating in a chaotic world.

So, my fellow cricket enthusiasts, these strategies for scoring runs bring excitement and ingenuity to the game. Whether it's rotating the strike, finding the gaps, unleashing power shots, targeting weaker bowlers, adapting to the situation, or displaying patience, these tactics showcase the strategic brilliance of cricket.

Next time you watch a match, observe how the batsmen employ these strategies to build partnerships, chase down targets, and set imposing totals. And if you find yourself on the cricket field, remember to mix the artistry of shot selection with the intelligence of game awareness, and you'll be well on your way to becoming a master run-scorer.

In the game of cricket, runs are the currency of success, and with these strategies in your arsenal, you'll be able to mint them with style and finesse. So, go out there, embrace the challenge, and let the runs flow like a refreshing waterfall in the scorching summer heat.

Playing Cricket: Bowling

Cricket, the gentleman's game, wouldn't be complete without the art of bowling. Below we will we'll explore the fascinating world of bowling and uncover the strategies and techniques employed by bowlers to bamboozle batsmen. Get ready for a journey filled with wickets, spin, and a touch of humor.

Firstly, let's discuss the importance of accuracy. Bowling is like trying to hit a bullseye on a dartboard while blindfolded. The bowler aims to deliver the ball with pinpoint accuracy, hitting the right length and line to trouble the batsman. It's like trying to thread a needle in a hurricane, but the skilled bowler manages to do it effortlessly.

Variety is the spice of bowling. It's like a magician pulling out different tricks from their hat. The bowler possesses a repertoire of deliveries, including fast-paced thunderbolts, cunning slower balls, and deceiving spin variations. It's a game of cat and mouse, where the bowler keeps the batsman guessing, just like a squirrel trying to outsmart a hungry fox.

Spin bowling adds a whole new dimension to the game. It's like a rollercoaster ride, with the ball spinning and twisting in the air and off the pitch. The spinner mesmerizes the batsman with their magical fingers, delivering balls that dance and drift, leaving the batsman in a state of bewilderment. It's a sight to behold, like watching a ballet performance on a cricket field.

Now, let's not forget the art of swing bowling. It's like a boomerang, with the ball curving through the air, defying gravity. The swing bowler generates movement by manipulating the seam and the air currents, making the ball dance through the atmosphere. It's a skill that requires finesse and precision, like a skilled archer hitting the bullseye from a hundred meters away.

Bowlers also employ clever strategies to outwit the batsman. It's like a game of chess, with each delivery a move on the board. They set traps, create illusions, and tempt the batsman into making a false move. It's a psychological battle, where the bowler tries to get into the mind of the batsman, like a mischievous imp playing mind games with its unsuspecting victim.

Bowling is not just about individual brilliance; it's also about teamwork. It's like a synchronized swimming routine, with fielders positioned strategically to support the bowler's efforts. They dive, leap, and catch with precision, ensuring that no ball goes to waste. It's a coordinated effort, like a well-drilled army executing a flawless battle plan.

Lastly, let's not forget the importance of perseverance. Bowling is like running a marathon; it requires stamina, determination, and the ability to bounce back after setbacks. The bowler faces challenges, such as batsmen hitting boundaries or surviving close calls, but they keep their chin up and continue the battle. It's a test of character, like a marathon runner pushing through the pain to reach the finish line.

So, my fellow cricket enthusiasts, bowling is an art form that adds excitement and unpredictability to the game. Whether it's accuracy, variety, spin, swing, strategy, teamwork, or perseverance, bowlers bring their unique style and skill to the cricket field.

Next time you watch a match, pay close attention to the bowlers and appreciate their craft. Observe the subtle variations, the cunning strategies, and the raw talent that goes into each delivery. And if you find yourself on the cricket field, remember to embrace the challenge, spin the ball like a magician, and swing it like a pendulum, and you'll be well on your way to becoming a formidable bowler.

In conclusion, bowling is the soul of cricket. It's the art of outfoxing batsmen, creating magical moments, and swinging the tide of the game. So, grab your ball, polish your skills, and let your bowling do the talking. Remember, in cricket, a well-executed delivery is worth a thousand words.

Bowling technique and delivery

Bowling in cricket is more than just a mere act of throwing a ball. It's an art form that requires skill, precision, and a touch of humor. Below we will we'll delve into the techniques and deliveries used by bowlers to bamboozle batsmen and keep the game exciting.

Firstly, let's talk about the grip. Holding the ball correctly is the foundation of a good delivery. It's like holding a slippery soap in the shower; you don't want it slipping out of your hands. The bowler's fingers play a crucial role in imparting spin, swing, or pace to the ball. They grip it with the finesse of a master chef delicately holding a cooking utensil.

Now, let's move on to the run-up. It's like a sprinter's dash, but with a ball in hand. The bowler charges in like a bull seeing red, building momentum to generate speed and power. It's a sight to behold, like watching a cheetah in full flight, but with a cricket ball instead of prey.

As the bowler approaches the crease, the delivery stride comes into play. It's like a ballet dancer's graceful movement, but with a touch of deception. The bowler changes pace, length, or angle to confuse the batsman. It's a bit like a magician's sleight of hand, making the batsman wonder where the ball will end up.

The release is the climax of the bowling action. It's like a catapult launching a projectile, only with finesse and precision. The bowler unleashes the ball with a flick of the wrist, using their fingers like a painter applying brush strokes to a canvas. It's a moment of sheer brilliance, like a firework exploding in the night sky.

Let's talk about the different types of deliveries. First, we have fast bowling. It's like a thunderstorm rolling in, with the ball hurtling towards the batsman at lightning speed. The fast bowler's aim is to rattle the batsman's confidence and send shivers down their spine, much like a rollercoaster ride with unexpected twists and turns.

Then, we have spin bowling. It's like a magician's trick, where the ball seems to change direction mid-air. The spin bowler imparts spin on the ball, causing it to deviate off the pitch. It's a bit like a merry-go-round, with the ball spinning and spinning, leaving the batsman dizzy and bewildered.

Let's not forget the art of swing bowling. It's like a boomerang in flight, curving through the air and surprising the batsman. The swing bowler uses the seam and atmospheric conditions to make the ball move in the air. It's like a dance partner leading their counterpart across the floor, with the batsman trying to keep up with the ball's unexpected movement.

Lastly, we have the yorker, the king of all deliveries. It's like a secret weapon, aimed at the batsman's toes. The bowler delivers the ball full and straight, making it difficult for the batsman to get their bat down in time. It's a bit like trying to stop a speeding train with a feather, nearly impossible.

In conclusion, bowling in cricket is an art that requires technique, skill, and a sprinkle of humor. From the grip to the run-up, the release to the different types of deliveries, bowlers bring excitement and uncertainty to the game. So, the next time you watch a cricket match, pay close attention to the bowlers and appreciate their craft. Remember, it's not just about throwing a ball; it's about the artistry and mastery that goes into each delivery.

Types of bowling styles

Cricket, the game of gentlemen (and gentlewomen), is known for its diverse range of bowling styles that add a touch of flair and intrigue to the sport. Below we will we will explore some of the most popular bowling styles in cricket, each with its own unique characteristics and a sprinkle of humor.

Firstly, we have the "Paceman." Just like a speeding bullet, the paceman generates blistering pace and sends the ball thundering towards the batsman. With a run-up resembling a bull charging at a matador, the paceman unleashes the ball with the ferocity of a lion pouncing on its prey. Batsmen face a daunting task of reacting swiftly, like a cat chasing a laser pointer, to defend against these fiery deliveries.

Next, we have the "Spinner." The spinner is like a magician with a bag of tricks, bamboozling batsmen with cunning spin and deceptive flight. With a run-up that resembles a gentle stroll in the park, the spinner's fingers work their magic on the ball, spinning it like a DJ spinning records at a party. Batsmen, in response, must navigate through the maze of spin, like a lost traveler trying to find their way in a labyrinth.

Another intriguing bowling style is the "Swing Bowler." Like a puppet master, the swing bowler has the ability to make the ball dance through the air. Using a combination of skill, seam position, and atmospheric conditions, the swing bowler swings the ball like a pendulum, leaving batsmen scratching their heads in bewilderment. It's like trying to hit a moving target with a blindfold on – a challenge that requires exceptional timing and coordination.

Let's not forget the "Seam Bowler." This crafty bowler uses the seam of the ball to exploit the pitch and deceive batsmen. With a run-up that resembles a cheetah stalking its prey, the seam bowler delivers the ball with pinpoint accuracy, making it deviate off the surface like a mischievous goblin. Batsmen must tread carefully, as even the slightest misjudgment can result in a wicket tumbling like a stack of cards.

A lesser-known but equally fascinating bowling style is the "Mystery Spinner." Like a Sherlock Holmes of the cricket field, the mystery spinner leaves batsmen scratching their heads in confusion. With unorthodox grips and unconventional deliveries, the mystery spinner seems to possess an enigmatic power that defies explanation. Batsmen, trying to solve this riddle, resemble a perplexed detective searching for clues.

Last but not least, we have the "Medium Pacer." This reliable and versatile bowler delivers medium-paced deliveries with accuracy and consistency. Like a tortoise in a race against the hare, the medium pacer relies on guile and control rather than sheer pace. They keep batsmen on their toes, patiently waiting for that one loose delivery to unleash their attacking shots.

In conclusion, cricket is a game filled with a myriad of bowling styles, each with its own charm and strategy. From the thunderous pace of the paceman to the mesmerizing spin of the spinner, bowlers bring excitement and unpredictability to the game. So, the next time you watch a cricket match, pay close attention to the bowlers and marvel at their mastery of different bowling styles. And remember, in cricket, just like in life, there's a bowling style for every occasion – all you need is a bit of skill, a dash of humor, and a love for the game.

Strategies for taking wickets

In the game of cricket, taking wickets is the ultimate goal for bowlers. It's like trying to collect rare Pokémon cards or catching that elusive fly buzzing around your room – challenging but immensely satisfying. Below we will we will explore some strategies that bowlers employ to outwit batsmen and claim those coveted wickets, all with a sprinkle of humor.

One effective strategy is the art of "swing bowling." Bowlers, like artists, use the seam position and atmospheric conditions to their advantage. By skillfully angling the seam and getting the ball to move in the air, bowlers create a visual spectacle that leaves batsmen scratching their heads. It's like playing a game of hide-and-seek with the ball, except the ball has a knack for disappearing just as you're about to hit it.

Another strategy is to induce a false sense of security with "change of pace." Like a magician pulling a rabbit out of a hat, bowlers surprise batsmen with slower deliveries that catch them off guard. It's like offering a tantalizing piece of cake, only to snatch it away at the last moment. Batsmen, in their eagerness to hit the ball, often find themselves caught out by the change in tempo.

Bowlers also rely on the power of "spin bowling." With a flick of the wrist and a twinkle in their eye, spinners send the ball on a delightful journey of spin and turn. It's like a dance between the ball and the pitch, with the batsman desperately trying to keep up. The key to success for spin bowlers lies in their ability to deceive batsmen with subtle variations in flight, pace, and spin – a game of cat and mouse where the mouse often finds itself in a spin.

In the quest for wickets, bowlers often resort to the strategy of "building pressure." Just like a pressure cooker, they gradually increase the intensity, making batsmen feel the heat. Tight lines, accurate lengths, and consistent deliveries create a sense of suffocation, causing batsmen to make rash decisions. It's like being trapped in a crowded elevator with no escape – the pressure builds, and mistakes are bound to happen.

Bowlers also capitalize on the power of "teamwork." They collaborate with fielders to set traps, just like a group of spies plotting an undercover mission. Fielders are strategically positioned, waiting to pounce on any opportunity that comes their way. It's like a game of chess, with bowlers and fielders moving their pieces strategically to corner the batsman.

Lastly, bowlers can rely on the element of surprise with "unorthodox deliveries." From the unpredictable "bouncer" that rises menacingly towards the batsman's head to the deceiving "yorker" that sneaks beneath the bat, unorthodox deliveries catch batsmen off guard. It's like a magic trick where the bowler pulls a rabbit out of the hat – or in this case, a wicket out of thin air.

In conclusion, taking wickets in cricket requires a combination of skill, strategy, and a sprinkle of humor. Bowlers employ a variety of tactics, from swing bowling and change of pace to spin bowling and building pressure. With teamwork, unorthodox deliveries, and a dash of surprise, bowlers aim to outwit batsmen and claim those precious wickets. So, the next time you watch a cricket match, pay close attention to the bowlers and their strategic maneuvers. And remember, in cricket, just like in life, sometimes a little humor can be the key to success – after all, laughter is the best wicket-taking medicine!

Playing Cricket: Fielding

In the game of cricket, while batting and bowling often steal the spotlight, fielding plays a crucial role in determining the outcome of a match. It's like the unsung hero of the game, quietly working behind the scenes to make those incredible catches and stops. Below we will we will explore the art of fielding in cricket, with a touch of humor to keep things entertaining.

Fielding in cricket is not just about standing around waiting for the ball to come to you – it's an active and dynamic role that requires skill, agility, and a keen eye. Fielders, like acrobats in a circus, need to be quick on their feet, ready to dive, slide, and leap to save runs and take wickets. It's like a game of Twister on a grassy field, where fielders twist and contort their bodies to make those extraordinary catches.

One of the key aspects of fielding is the art of "catching." Fielders become the superheroes of the game, soaring through the air like caped crusaders to pluck the ball out of thin air. It's like a high-stakes game of fetch, with the fielder determined to outwit the batsman and bring the ball safely into their hands. Spectacular catches not only mesmerize the crowd but also demoralize the batsman, leaving them wondering if they're facing cricket players or human spider-men.

Fielders also exhibit their prowess through "ground fielding." Like graceful ballet dancers, they glide across the field, their nimble feet making swift movements to stop the ball from reaching the boundary. It's like a game of tag, where the fielder tries to tag the ball with their hands before it escapes their grasp. The sight of a perfectly executed slide to save a boundary is enough to make even the most stoic of spectators gasp in awe.

The importance of communication cannot be overlooked in fielding. Fielders are like a close-knit team, sharing secret codes and whispers to outsmart the batsmen. It's like a covert operation, where fielders use coded signals to indicate their strategy and confuse the batsman. A well-coordinated run-out is the ultimate reward of this covert communication – a moment of triumph that sends shockwaves through the stadium.

Fielders also display their throwing skills, like expert javelin throwers aiming for the bullseye. From long-distance throws to hit the stumps and run out batsmen to quick releases to prevent runs, fielders showcase their accuracy and precision. It's like a game of darts, where the fielder's throw determines the fate of the game. A direct hit on the stumps is a moment of pure joy, like hitting the bullseye and winning the jackpot.

In conclusion, fielding in cricket is an art that requires skill, agility, and excellent communication. Fielders become the unsung heroes of the game, making remarkable catches, stopping boundaries, and executing run-outs. Their acrobatic moves, precision throws, and covert communication tactics add excitement and drama to the game. So, the next time you watch a cricket match, pay close attention to the fielders and their incredible feats – you may just witness a display of athleticism that leaves you in awe. After all, in cricket, fielding is not just a job – it's an opportunity to shine and make your mark on the field.

Fielding positions and roles

In the game of cricket, fielding positions and roles are as diverse as the flavors in an ice cream parlor. Each fielding position has its unique responsibilities and plays a crucial role in the team's strategy. So, let's take a comical stroll through the cricket field and explore the various positions and their amusing roles.

First up is the wicketkeeper, often referred to as the "behind-the-stumps ninja." Equipped with gloves and pads, this player crouches like a stealthy ninja behind the wicket, ready to pounce on any opportunity. Their primary role is to catch the ball when the batsman misses or edges it, while simultaneously trying to stump them out by whipping off the bails. It's like a game of Whac-A-Mole, where the wicketkeeper tries to react faster than a speeding bullet and send the batsman back to the pavilion.

Next, we have the slip fielders, who stand close to the batsman and form a human wall of defense. These brave souls resemble the characters from a thriller movie, always on high alert for any edge or deflection. Their job is to catch those sneaky edges that elude the wicketkeeper. It's like a game of "catch me if you can," where the slip fielders use their lightning-fast reflexes to snatch the ball just inches from the ground, leaving the batsman stunned.

Moving on to the outfield positions, we encounter the boundary riders – the guardians of the boundary rope. Positioned near the boundary, they resemble superheroes patrolling the city, ready to leap into action. Their task is to prevent the ball from crossing the boundary and save valuable runs. It's like a game of tag, where the boundary riders chase after the ball, dive, and somersault to keep it in play. Sometimes, they even perform gravity-defying acts to pluck the ball out of thin air, much to the astonishment of the spectators.

Let's not forget the fielders in the deep, strategically placed to stop those mighty sixes. They're like treasure hunters guarding buried treasure. With a keen eye and a swift arm, they aim to retrieve the ball and hurl it back to the infield. It's like a game of fetch, where the fielder tries to outsmart the batsman by reaching the ball before it escapes into the crowd. The fielders in the deep have to be cautious not to stumble over their own feet, as they navigate the tricky terrain near the boundary.

Last but not least, we have the close-in fielders, standing perilously close to the batsman. They're like the batsman's personal space invaders, constantly testing their nerves. Their job is to prevent the batsman from scoring easy singles and to create pressure by maintaining a strong presence. It's like a game of psychological warfare, where the close-in fielders try to intimidate the batsman with their close proximity and menacing stares.

In conclusion, fielding positions in cricket are like characters in a theater production, each with their own unique role and contribution to the team. From the nimble wicketkeeper to the agile boundary riders, every fielder plays a part in the grand cricketing spectacle. So, the next time you watch a cricket match, pay attention to the fielders and their amusing roles – you might just find yourself laughing along with their comical antics. After all, in cricket, fielding is not just about stopping the ball – it's about adding excitement and entertainment to the game.

Catching and throwing techniques

In the world of cricket, catching and throwing are like the dynamic duo, working together to create moments of pure joy and astonishment. So, grab your cricket gear and let's dive into the art of catching and throwing techniques, sprinkled with a touch of humor.

When it comes to catching, the cricket field transforms into a stage for acrobats and contortionists. Picture a flying circus troupe, gracefully soaring through the air, attempting to pluck the ball out of the sky. Catching requires a combination of agility, timing, and bravery. Fielders position themselves with arms outstretched, like superheroes ready to intercept the ball. They leap, twist, and sometimes even defy gravity to complete the catch. It's like a game of "catch me if you can," where fielders make the most extraordinary grabs, leaving everyone in awe. However, occasionally, even the best fielders have their clumsy moments, resulting in amusing fumbles that elicit laughter from the crowd.

Now, let's shift our focus to throwing, an art that can make or break a fielder's reputation. The aim is to unleash the ball like a superhero's projectile, accurately and with lightning speed. Fielders employ various throwing techniques to achieve this feat. There's the classic overarm throw, reminiscent of a javelin thrower's motion. It requires precision and a touch of finesse to hit the target with accuracy. Then there's the sidearm throw, resembling a cricketer attempting a sneaky underarm delivery. This technique is perfect for quick, low trajectory throws, catching the batsman off guard. And let's not forget the occasional "hail-Mary" throw, where the fielder launches the ball as far as possible, hoping it reaches the wicketkeeper or a teammate. It's like a game of darts, where fielders aim for the bullseye, except the bullseye is a set of stumps or a teammate's waiting hands.

Catching and throwing are not just about physical prowess; they involve mental sharpness as well. Fielders have to anticipate the trajectory of the ball, calculate the distance, and make split-second decisions. It's like playing a game of chess, where fielders strategize and position themselves strategically to intercept the ball. The ability to judge the ball's speed and direction is vital, much like predicting the weather (well, maybe not that accurate!).

Let's not forget the occasional mishaps that occur on the field. Misjudging the ball's trajectory can result in hilarious and embarrassing moments. Fielders dive and tumble like a clumsy clown, only to see the ball bouncing away untouched. It's like a scene from a slapstick comedy, where everyone has a good laugh, including the fielder who becomes the unwitting star of the show.

In conclusion, catching and throwing in cricket are a blend of athleticism, skill, and entertainment. Fielders perform astonishing catches that leave spectators in awe and showcase their agility and bravery. The art of throwing requires precision and a touch of showmanship to deliver the ball accurately to its destination. But amidst the incredible moments, there are also amusing mishaps that remind us that even the best fielders can have their off days. So, the next time you watch a cricket match, keep an eye on the fielders as they dive, leap, and throw with gusto. You might witness a breathtaking catch or a comical blunder, both of which add a sprinkle of humor to the beautiful game of cricket.

Strategies for stopping runs

Cricket, like any good game, is a battle between two forces: the batsmen trying to score runs and the fielding team desperately trying to stop them. In this entertaining and informative piece, we will explore some clever strategies fielders employ to prevent those pesky runs from accumulating on the scoreboard, all while sprinkling a little humor into the mix.

First and foremost, fielders must be like ninjas, lurking in the shadows, ready to pounce on any opportunity to halt the flow of runs. They strategically position themselves on the field, taking advantage of the batsmen's weaknesses. It's like playing a game of chess, where fielders anticipate the batsman's moves and react accordingly. The goal is to create an impenetrable wall, a fortress where runs go to die.

One of the primary strategies fielders use is aggressive field placements. They position themselves closer to the batsmen, daring them to take risky shots. It's like setting a trap, enticing the batsman to go for glory but leaving them vulnerable to getting caught out. Fielders in catching positions are like spiders, patiently waiting for their prey to make a fatal mistake.

Another effective strategy is tight bowling and fielding. Fielders need to be agile and quick as gazelles, swooping down on the ball like hungry predators. By restricting the batsman's scoring options, fielders put pressure on them to take unnecessary risks. It's like a game of poker, where fielders bluff the batsman into making a reckless move, resulting in their downfall.

Fielders also employ the art of deception. They lure batsmen into false security by giving them a false sense of opportunity. They might intentionally leave gaps in the field, tempting the batsman to take a risky single or go for a big shot. But as soon as the ball is struck, the fielders pounce like cheetahs, swiftly closing the gaps and denying the run. It's like a magician's trick, where the audience is led to believe one thing, only to be left astounded by the unexpected outcome.

Communication and teamwork play a vital role in stopping runs. Fielders need to be like a synchronized dance troupe, constantly communicating with each other, ensuring they cover all angles. It's like a well-orchestrated symphony, where each player knows their role and timing. Miscommunication can lead to hilarious mix-ups, with fielders colliding and the ball slipping through their fingers, much to the amusement of the crowd.

Fielders must also be alert and quick thinkers. They need to be ready to seize every opportunity to run out a batsman. It's like playing a game of tag, where fielders chase the batsmen, aiming to tag them out before they reach the crease. The thrill of a run-out is like catching a lightning bolt in a bottle, leaving everyone gasping in awe.

In conclusion, stopping runs in cricket is an art form, blending strategy, athleticism, and teamwork. Fielders strategically position themselves, employ aggressive field placements, and tighten the screws on the batsmen through tight bowling and fielding. They use deception and communication to outwit their opponents and seize every opportunity to run them out. And amidst all the serious tactics, there are moments of hilarity and amusement when things don't go according to plan. So, the next time you watch a cricket match, keep an eye on the fielders as they execute these clever strategies, and don't forget to appreciate the humorous mishaps that add a sprinkle of fun to the game.

Cricket Formats and Competitions

Cricket, the sport that has captured the hearts of millions, offers a variety of formats and competitions to cater to different tastes and preferences. From the classic Test matches that stretch over five days to the fast-paced excitement of Twenty20 cricket, there is something for everyone. In this informative and humor-infused piece, we will explore the various cricket formats and competitions that keep fans on the edge of their seats.

Let's start with the granddaddy of them all, Test cricket. It's like the marathon of the cricketing world, testing the endurance and skills of players over five grueling days. Fans often joke that watching a Test match can be a test of their patience too. But there is a certain charm in witnessing the ebb and flow of the game, the strategic battles between batsmen and bowlers, and the suspense that builds up over days. It's like a slow-burning novel, where the climax is worth the wait.

For those who prefer a shorter, more action-packed format, One Day Internationals (ODIs) are the perfect choice. With a limited number of overs, usually 50, teams need to strike a balance between building a solid foundation and going for big hits. It's like a roller coaster ride, where the tension keeps rising with every boundary and wicket. And of course, who can forget the nail-biting finishes that often leave fans biting their nails and tearing their hair out?

In recent years, Twenty20 cricket has taken the cricketing world by storm. This format is like the energy drink of cricket, providing an explosive burst of excitement in just 20 overs per side. It's a batsman's paradise, where big hits and innovative shots take center stage. Bowlers have to be crafty and come up with ingenious ways to deceive the batsmen. And in the field, fielders must be agile like acrobats, diving and leaping to stop those boundary shots. Twenty20 cricket is like a firecracker, exploding with entertainment and leaving spectators wanting more.

On the international stage, we have the prestigious ICC Cricket World Cup. It's like the Olympics of cricket, where nations from around the globe compete for the ultimate prize. The World Cup unites fans and players alike, creating an atmosphere of camaraderie and intense rivalry. It's like a grand feast, where cricketing nations showcase their skills and battle for supremacy. The World Cup has produced countless unforgettable moments, from spectacular catches to stunning batting performances, etching themselves into the annals of cricketing history.

At the domestic level, each country has its own professional cricket league, where players showcase their talent and entertain fans. The Indian Premier League (IPL) is the epitome of glitz and glamour, with its star-studded lineups and fierce rivalries. It's like a Bollywood blockbuster, complete with drama, emotions, and dazzling performances. Other countries also have their own domestic leagues, such as the Big Bash League (BBL) in Australia and the Vitality Blast in England, providing local fans with a chance to cheer for their favorite teams.

In conclusion, cricket offers a smorgasbord of formats and competitions, catering to the diverse tastes of fans around the world. Whether you enjoy the timeless battles of Test cricket, the thrill of ODIs, the explosive excitement of Twenty20 cricket, or the global spectacle of the Cricket World Cup, there is always something to keep you entertained. So, grab your popcorn, settle in, and prepare for a cricketing extravaganza filled with humor, drama, and moments that will make you jump out of your seat.

Test cricket

Ah, Test cricket, the ultimate test of skill, endurance, and patience in the world of cricket. It's the format that separates the true cricket aficionados from the casual fans. Picture this: five days of cricket, teams battling it out under the scorching sun, players in white uniforms, and spectators engrossed in the ebb and flow of the game. It's a unique blend of strategy, technique, and mental fortitude that sets Test cricket apart.

In Test cricket, teams play two innings each, giving both the batting and bowling sides a chance to shine. It's like a marathon, where players need to pace themselves and carefully strategize their approach. The pitch undergoes wear and tear over the course of five days, evolving into a challenging battlefield for both batsmen and bowlers. It's like a game of chess, where each move is carefully planned and executed.

One of the unique aspects of Test cricket is the concept of 'declaring.' Picture this scenario: a team has amassed a massive total, and the captain decides to end the innings and give the opposition a chance to bat. It's like saying, "Alright, we've had our fun, now it's your turn to face the music." This strategic move adds a layer of excitement and unpredictability to the game, as teams try to outwit each other and make the most of their opportunities.

Another intriguing aspect of Test cricket is the role of the weather. Oh, the weather, the bane of many cricket matches. Rain delays and bad light can throw a spanner in the works, forcing players and fans to anxiously monitor the skies. It's like a game of hide and seek with the weather gods, where everyone prays for clear skies and uninterrupted play. But hey, sometimes rain delays give players a chance to catch their breath and fans a chance to stock up on snacks.

And let's not forget the iconic Ashes series between England and Australia. It's like a family feud that has spanned over a century. The Ashes is a test of national pride and rivalry, with both teams leaving no stone unturned in their quest for victory. It's like a tug of war, each team tugging at the Ashes urn with all their might, hoping to claim bragging rights for years to come.

But amidst all the excitement and drama, Test cricket has a certain elegance and grace to it. It's a format that allows players to showcase their true skills and adaptability. Batsmen need to display patience and concentration, carefully building their innings brick by brick. Bowlers need to vary their line and length, utilizing swing, spin, and pace to outfox the batsmen. It's like a dance, with the players gracefully moving across the field, showcasing their talent and athleticism.

In conclusion, Test cricket is the epitome of the gentleman's game. It's a format that tests the skills, endurance, and mental fortitude of players. With its strategic battles, unpredictable weather, and iconic rivalries, Test cricket offers a unique spectacle for cricket enthusiasts around the world. So, grab your tea, settle into your favorite armchair, and prepare for five days of captivating cricket that will keep you on the edge of your seat, wondering what twists and turns await.

One Day International (ODI) cricket

Ah, One Day International (ODI) cricket, the format that brings excitement, thrill, and a sense of urgency to the game. Picture this: teams battling it out in colorful jerseys, spectators cheering and waving flags, and players striving to score runs and take wickets within a limited number of overs. It's like a race against time, where every ball counts and every run matters.

In ODI cricket, each team gets a maximum of 50 overs to showcase their skills and amass runs on the scoreboard. It's like a game of cricket on fast-forward, where players need to find the perfect balance between aggression and caution. There's no time for leisurely tea breaks or long-drawn-out battles; it's all about action-packed entertainment.

One of the fascinating aspects of ODI cricket is the use of white balls. Yes, you heard that right. In a format that demands fast-paced action, the traditional red cricket ball takes a backseat and is replaced by its white counterpart. It's like the ball saying, "Hey, I'm ready to party and light up the field!" Plus, white balls are easier to spot under floodlights, making night-time cricket a visual spectacle.

Now, let's talk about fielding restrictions. In the early stages of an ODI innings, fielding teams are allowed a limited number of fielders outside the inner circle. It's like a game of hide and seek, where batsmen try to find gaps and score boundaries while fielding teams try to close in and prevent easy runs. These restrictions add a strategic element to the game, forcing captains and bowlers to make calculated decisions on field placements.

Oh, and who can forget the dreaded Duckworth-Lewis-Stern (DLS) method? When rain interrupts play, this mathematical formula comes into play, calculating revised targets for the batting side. It's like solving a complex equation while players anxiously check the sky for any signs of rain. Sometimes, the DLS method can turn the tide of the game, creating nail-biting finishes and adding a dash of unpredictability.

One of the highlights of ODI cricket is the coveted ICC Cricket World Cup. Held every four years, it brings together teams from around the world, competing for the ultimate prize. It's like a global carnival of cricket, where fans unite, flags fly high, and nations hold their breath in anticipation. The World Cup is a platform for heroes to emerge, records to be broken, and unforgettable moments to be etched in cricketing history.

In conclusion, ODI cricket is a thrilling and action-packed format that keeps fans on the edge of their seats. With limited overs, white balls, fielding restrictions, and the excitement of the ICC Cricket World Cup, ODI cricket offers a perfect blend of skill, strategy, and entertainment. So, grab your popcorn, get your vuvuzelas ready, and prepare for a rollercoaster ride of boundaries, wickets, and heart-stopping moments that will leave you craving for more. After all, in ODI cricket, every ball has the potential to change the game, and every run brings the crowd to its feet.

Twenty20 (T20) cricket

Ah, Twenty20 (T20) cricket, the format that brings all the thrill and excitement of cricket in a compact and explosive package. It's like cricket's version of a power-packed blockbuster movie, where every ball has the potential to be a game-changer and every shot can make the crowd go wild.

In T20 cricket, each team gets a maximum of 20 overs to showcase their batting prowess, score as many runs as possible, and set a daunting target for their opponents. It's like a high-stakes poker game, where players go all-in from the start, unleashing their attacking shots and strategic maneuvers to outsmart the opposition.

One of the most noticeable features of T20 cricket is the fast-paced nature of the game. Bowlers need to be on their toes, trying to deceive batsmen with their variations, while batsmen look to unleash a flurry of boundaries and sixes. It's like a race against time, where every second counts and every run matters.

Now, let's talk about the batting pyrotechnics in T20 cricket. It's a format where players are encouraged to go big or go home. Shots like the "helicopter shot" made famous by MS Dhoni or the "dil-scoop" pioneered by Tillakaratne Dilshan become the talk of the town. It's like witnessing a fireworks display, with batsmen showcasing their innovative shot-making skills and leaving spectators in awe.

Fielding in T20 cricket is no less thrilling. Players dive, slide, and stretch to save every run. It's like watching acrobats in action, defying gravity to take breathtaking catches or execute lightning-fast run-outs. Fielders become superheroes, soaring through the air to pluck the ball out of thin air or unleash rocket-like throws to hit the stumps.

Now, let's not forget about the T20 cricket leagues that have taken the world by storm. The Indian Premier League (IPL), Big Bash League (BBL), and Caribbean Premier League (CPL) are just a few examples of the glitz, glamour, and entertainment that T20 cricket brings to the table. It's like a cricketing carnival, where international stars team up with local talents, and fans cheer and dance in the stands.

But amidst all the excitement and entertainment, T20 cricket also demands strategic thinking. Captains and coaches have to make quick decisions, analyzing match situations, and adapting their game plans accordingly. It's like playing a game of chess at lightning speed, where each move has to be calculated and executed flawlessly.

In conclusion, T20 cricket is a thrilling, high-energy format that brings together the best of batting, bowling, and fielding in a whirlwind of excitement. With its explosive shots, nail-biting finishes, and star-studded leagues, T20 cricket has captivated audiences worldwide and redefined the way the game is played. So, grab your popcorn, put on your team's jersey, and get ready to witness the fireworks and drama that only T20 cricket can deliver. After all, in T20 cricket, it's not just about the game; it's about the entertainment and the memories that will last a lifetime.

Major international competitions

Cricket, the gentleman's game, has produced some of the most thrilling and iconic international competitions that keep fans on the edge of their seats. These tournaments are like the grand stage where teams from different nations battle it out to claim cricketing supremacy. It's like the Olympics of cricket, where national pride and bragging rights are at stake.

One of the most prestigious tournaments in cricket is the ICC Cricket World Cup. Held every four years, this event brings together the best teams from around the globe. It's like the ultimate showdown, where cricketing giants clash and nations hold their breath in anticipation. The World Cup is a spectacle of skill, strategy, and drama that has produced unforgettable moments like the legendary six by MS Dhoni in the 2011 final.

Another international competition that has its own charm is the ICC Champions Trophy. Often called the "mini-World Cup," it features the top-ranked cricketing nations battling it out in a shorter format. It's like a compact version of the World Cup, where teams showcase their talent and fight for glory. The Champions Trophy has witnessed nail-biting finishes, unexpected upsets, and breathtaking performances that keep fans hooked till the last ball.

Now, let's not forget about the fierce rivalry between England and Australia in The Ashes. This historic Test series, played between the two cricketing giants, is like a battle for pride and honor. The series dates back to 1882 when Australia defeated England on English soil, and a mock obituary declared that English cricket had died, giving birth to The Ashes. It's like a long-standing feud, with both teams fighting tooth and nail to win the coveted urn.

In the realm of T20 cricket, we have the ICC World Twenty20, a tournament that brings the excitement and thrill of the shortest format to a global stage. It's like a party where every team showcases their power-hitting skills, bowling variations, and acrobatic fielding. The World Twenty20 is a carnival of boundaries, sixes, and electrifying moments that leave fans mesmerized.

Now, let's shift our attention to regional competitions. In India, the Indian Premier League (IPL) takes center stage. It's like a cricketing extravaganza, where international superstars team up with local talents, creating a melting pot of talent and entertainment. The IPL has its own fanfare, with cheerleaders, music, and Bollywood celebrities adding to the glitz and glamour.

In the Caribbean, we have the Caribbean Premier League (CPL), a tournament that captures the spirit of the islands with its vibrant atmosphere and pulsating cricket. It's like a party on the beach, where players bring their flair and style to the game, and fans dance to the rhythm of calypso beats.

In conclusion, cricket is not just a sport; it's a stage for intense competitions that unite nations and captivate fans worldwide. From the ICC Cricket World Cup to The Ashes and the IPL to the CPL, these tournaments showcase the best of cricket and provide moments of joy, heartbreak, and celebration. So, grab your cricket bat, put on your team's jersey, and get ready to witness the battles, rivalries, and triumphs that make cricket an extraordinary sport. And remember, in cricket, anything can happen, and the game is always full of surprises.

Understanding Cricket Strategy

Cricket, the game known for its strategic depth, requires more than just skillful batting and bowling. It's a game of strategy, where captains and players have to make tactical decisions to outsmart their opponents. From field placements to bowling changes, cricket strategy adds a layer of excitement and unpredictability to the game. So, let's unravel the intriguing world of cricket strategy with a touch of humor.

One of the most crucial aspects of cricket strategy is field placement. The captain strategically positions fielders to maximize the chances of getting a wicket or limiting the scoring opportunities of the batting team. It's like a game of chess, where every fielder has a role to play. The slips are like the knights, waiting for an edge to pounce on, while the fielders in the outfield cover the ground like rooks guarding their territory.

Bowling changes are another strategic move in cricket. Captains have to carefully analyze the game situation and decide when to introduce different bowlers. It's like a buffet, where the captain brings out different flavors to keep the batsmen guessing. Spinners are like the chefs who add a dash of mystery and deception to their deliveries, while fast bowlers are like the waiters who serve up fiery spells.

The powerplay overs in limited-overs cricket are like the happy hour at a bar. The batting team tries to maximize their scoring during this period when only a limited number of fielders are allowed outside the circle. It's like a race against time to stack up the runs before the field spreads out, and the party ends. On the other hand, the bowling team aims to break through and take wickets during this phase, like bouncers that catch you off guard when you least expect it.

In cricket, reviews have become an integral part of the game. It's like calling for a second opinion when you can't decide if the pizza is perfectly cooked or undercooked. Captains and players use the Decision Review System (DRS) to challenge umpiring decisions. Sometimes it's like a game of poker, where players make a calculated gamble, hoping the review will turn the tide in their favor. And when the review goes wrong, it's like ordering a dish that turns out to be a spicy surprise.

Run-chases in cricket require a different set of strategies. The batting team has to balance aggression and caution, like a game of tug-of-war where they constantly assess the target and the available resources. It's like trying to finish a meal before the restaurant closes, where you have to pace yourself and make strategic choices to reach your goal.

Lastly, cricket strategy also involves mind games and sledging. Players try to get under each other's skin through witty banter and humorous remarks. It's like a comedy show where the players become stand-up comedians, trying to distract their opponents with their quick wit and humor. But at the end of the day, it's all part of the game, and friendships are often formed off the field.

In conclusion, cricket strategy adds a fascinating layer to the game, where captains and players use their tactical acumen to gain an edge over their opponents. From field placements to bowling changes and run-chase calculations, cricket strategy is like a complex puzzle that keeps evolving with every delivery. So, next time you watch a cricket match, pay close attention to the mind games, the field settings, and the bowling variations. And remember, cricket is not just a battle of skills, but also a battle of wits and strategies.

Batting strategy

Batting in cricket is both an art and a science. It requires skill, technique, and a strategic approach to score runs and build a solid innings. From shot selection to reading the field placements, batting strategy plays a crucial role in determining a team's success. So, let's delve into the world of batting strategy with a sprinkle of humor.

One of the key aspects of batting strategy is shot selection. Batsmen have a wide array of shots at their disposal, and choosing the right shot at the right time is like picking the perfect toppings for a pizza. It's a delicate balance between aggression and caution. Playing an extravagant shot is like adding extra cheese, it can be deliciously satisfying, but it also comes with the risk of getting caught out. On the other hand, playing a defensive shot is like ordering a plain margherita, it may not be as flashy, but it ensures safety and survival.

Reading the field placements is another important aspect of batting strategy. The fielders are like obstacles on a mini-golf course, strategically positioned to thwart the batsmen's scoring opportunities. Batsmen have to identify the gaps in the field and find ways to pierce through them. It's like aiming for the perfect hole-in-one, with fielders acting as sneaky windmills trying to block your path. Finding the gaps is like discovering a secret passage to a treasure trove of runs.

Building partnerships is crucial in cricket, and it requires a collaborative batting strategy. Batsmen have to communicate, understand each other's strengths and weaknesses, and rotate the strike. It's like a dance partnership, where one partner leads while the other supports and follows. And just like in a dance routine, timing and coordination are key. A well-built partnership is like a synchronized performance, where runs flow like smooth dance moves.

Adjusting to different bowling styles is another aspect of batting strategy. It's like encountering different flavors of ice cream. Some bowlers are like fiery chili-infused scoops that make your taste buds tingle, while others are like subtle vanilla flavors that require patience and concentration. Batsmen have to adapt their technique and shot selection to counter different bowling styles, just like trying different ice cream flavors and adjusting your licking technique accordingly.

Knowing when to accelerate the run-rate is crucial in limited-overs cricket. It's like deciding when to leave the safety of the harbor and set sail for a daring adventure. Batsmen have to assess the game situation, calculate the risks, and determine the right time to play aggressive shots and score quick runs. It's like raising the anchor and setting a course towards a big total, with fielders chasing after the runs like seagulls after fish and chips.

In conclusion, batting strategy in cricket is a combination of skill, decision-making, and adaptability. Batsmen have to choose their shots wisely, read the field placements, build partnerships, adjust to different bowling styles, and make calculated decisions to score runs and contribute to their team's success. Just like a good cook, batsmen have to mix the ingredients of technique, shot selection, and game awareness to create a winning recipe. So, the next time you watch a cricket match, pay attention to the batting strategies employed by the players and marvel at their ability to navigate the challenges thrown at them by the opposing team. And who knows, you might even pick up a few batting tips to improve your own game.

Bowling strategy

Bowling in cricket is like being a magician on the field. It requires skill, variation, and a strategic approach to outwit the batsmen and take wickets. From selecting the right delivery to setting up the batsmen, bowling strategy plays a crucial role in determining a team's success. So, let's step into the shoes of a bowler and explore the world of bowling strategy with a sprinkle of humor.

One of the key aspects of bowling strategy is the selection of deliveries. Bowlers have a repertoire of deliveries, each with its own tricks up its sleeve. It's like being a chef with a variety of spices to add to your cooking. A well-executed yorker is like a pinch of salt, it adds the perfect touch to the dish and catches the batsman off-guard. A slower ball is like a dash of chili powder, it deceives the batsman with its change of pace and leaves them in a fiery mess. The key is to use the right delivery at the right time, just like adding the right spice to create a mouth-watering dish.

Bowlers also need to be strategic in setting up the batsmen. It's like playing a game of chess, where every move is calculated to put the opponent in checkmate. Bowlers have to assess the batsman's strengths and weaknesses, study their shot selection, and plan their bowling accordingly. It's like baiting a fish with a juicy worm, luring the batsman into making a false move and then striking with a well-disguised delivery. The thrill of outsmarting the batsman is like shouting "Checkmate!" and watching their puzzled expression.

Bowling partnerships are essential in cricket. It's like being part of a comedy duo, where one bowler sets up the joke and the other delivers the punchline. The bowlers have to work in tandem, creating pressure from both ends and taking turns to attack and defend. It's like a well-rehearsed comedy routine, where the batsmen become the audience waiting for the next twist and turn. And just like in comedy, timing and chemistry between the bowlers are crucial for a successful partnership.

Adapting to different game situations is another aspect of bowling strategy. It's like being a chameleon, changing colors to blend into different environments. Bowlers have to adjust their line, length, and pace based on the pitch conditions, the state of the game, and the batsmen's form. It's like switching gears in a car, knowing when to accelerate and when to apply the brakes. Adapting to the situation is like a magician pulling out different tricks from their hat, keeping the batsmen guessing and on their toes.

Knowing the batsman's weaknesses and exploiting them is a key element of bowling strategy. It's like finding the Achilles' heel of a superhero. Bowlers study the batsman's technique, their preferred shots, and their vulnerable areas. It's like discovering that the superhero is weak against a particular element, and then using it to your advantage. A well-executed plan to exploit a batsman's weakness is like finding the perfect weapon to defeat the superhero and claim victory.

In conclusion, bowling strategy in cricket is a blend of skill, cunning, and adaptability. Bowlers have to select the right deliveries, set up the batsmen, build partnerships with fellow bowlers, adapt to different game situations, and exploit the batsmen's weaknesses. Just like a magician, they have to mesmerize the audience with their variations and tricks. So, the next time you watch a cricket match, pay attention to the bowling strategies employed by the players and marvel at their ability to outfox the batsmen. And who knows, you might even pick up a few tricks to bamboozle your friends in your next backyard cricket game.

Fielding strategy

Fielding in cricket is not just about stopping the ball or taking catches; it's an art of its own. A good fielding strategy can turn the game around and put immense pressure on the opposition. So, let's dive into the world of fielding strategy with a touch of humor and explore how fielders play a vital role in cricket.

One of the key aspects of fielding strategy is positioning the fielders. It's like playing a game of chess, where every move is calculated to anticipate the batsman's shots. Fielders need to be strategically placed to cut off boundaries and create pressure on the batsman. It's like setting up a series of booby traps, making the batsman feel like they're walking through a minefield. The anticipation and excitement of seeing the batsman fall into the trap is like watching a hilarious prank unfold.

Communication among fielders is crucial for a successful fielding strategy. It's like being part of a secret agent team, where signals and codes are used to convey important information. Fielders have to communicate their positions, give instructions, and coordinate their movements to prevent runs and take catches. It's like a well-choreographed dance routine, where everyone moves in sync and the batsman is left bewildered by the seamless coordination.

Fielders need to be agile and quick on their feet. It's like being a ninja, dodging the batsman's shots and making acrobatic saves. They have to dive, slide, and leap to stop the ball from reaching the boundary. It's like performing a series of gravity-defying stunts, leaving the audience in awe of their athleticism. And just like in a comedy movie, the fielder's hilarious tumble after making a spectacular save adds an element of humor to the game.

Fielders also need to be aware of the batsman's strengths and weaknesses. It's like being a detective, studying the batsman's shot selection and predicting their next move. Fielders position themselves strategically to exploit the batsman's weaknesses and force them into making mistakes. It's like leading the batsman into a trap with a trail of breadcrumbs, only to catch them off-guard with a brilliant fielding effort. The satisfaction of executing a well-thought-out plan is like solving a complex mystery and unveiling the culprit.

Fielders have to be quick in retrieving the ball and returning it to the wicketkeeper or bowler. It's like being a superhero with super speed, zooming in to rescue the ball and prevent the batsman from scoring extra runs. They have to throw accurately and swiftly, like a superhero launching a powerful attack on the villain. And just like in a superhero movie, a perfectly timed throw that results in a run-out brings cheers from the crowd and a touch of humor when the batsman's expression is caught on the big screen.

In conclusion, fielding strategy in cricket is a combination of positioning, communication, agility, and awareness. Fielders have to be strategically placed, communicate effectively, showcase their athleticism, exploit the batsman's weaknesses, and execute quick and accurate throws. It's like a well-coordinated comedy act, where the fielders play their roles to perfection and entertain the audience with their fielding prowess. So, the next time you watch a cricket match, pay attention to the fielding strategies employed by the players and appreciate the humor and skill they bring to the game. And who knows, you might even pick up a few tricks to showcase your own fielding heroics in your next backyard cricket match.

Team strategy

Cricket is not just an individual sport; it's a team effort that requires coordination, strategy, and a good sense of humor. Let's explore the world of team strategy in cricket and discover how teams come together to outwit their opponents and create memorable moments on the field.

One of the most important aspects of team strategy is selecting the right combination of players. It's like assembling a group of superheroes with unique powers and abilities. Each player brings something special to the team, whether it's explosive batting, accurate bowling, or exceptional fielding. It's like forming a superhero squad, where everyone has a role to play and contributes to the team's success. And just like in a superhero movie, the banter and camaraderie between teammates adds a touch of humor to the game.

Team strategy also involves setting goals and plans for each game. It's like devising a master plan to conquer the enemy's fortress. The team discusses tactics, analyzes the opposition's strengths and weaknesses, and formulates strategies to exploit them. It's like plotting a heist, where every move is calculated, and surprises are sprung at the right moment. The excitement and suspense of executing the team's strategy is like watching a thrilling action movie unfold.

Communication is key in team strategy. Players need to communicate on the field, share insights, and support each other. It's like a secret agent operation, where coded messages and signals are used to convey important information. The team has to be in sync, like a well-oiled machine, to execute plans flawlessly. And just like in a spy movie, the witty banter and inside jokes among teammates keep the atmosphere light-hearted and fun.

Adaptability is another crucial aspect of team strategy. Cricket is a game that can change rapidly, and teams need to be flexible in their approach. It's like a comedy improvisation show, where the players have to think on their feet and adjust their strategies based on the changing game situation. They have to be quick to adapt, like comedians coming up with funny punchlines on the spot. The ability to handle unexpected situations with humor and grace can often turn the game in their favor.

Team spirit plays a significant role in team strategy. It's like being part of a close-knit family, where players support and uplift each other. They celebrate victories together and provide a shoulder to lean on during tough times. It's like the cast of a comedy TV show, where the chemistry and camaraderie among the characters create hilarious and heartwarming moments. The joy and laughter shared within the team not only strengthen the bond but also boost morale and performance.

In conclusion, team strategy is an essential aspect of cricket. It involves selecting the right players, setting goals and plans, effective communication, adaptability, and fostering team spirit. Cricket teams are like a group of superheroes, devising strategies, executing plans, and entertaining the audience with their skills and humor. So, the next time you watch a cricket match, pay attention to the team dynamics and the strategies employed. You'll witness the power of teamwork and the impact it can have on the game. And who knows, you might even pick up a few comedic tricks to bring laughter to your own team endeavors.

Cricket Skills Development

Cricket is a game that requires a unique set of skills, and developing those skills is a journey filled with challenges, dedication, and a pinch of humor. Let's dive into the world of cricket skills development and discover how players master the art of batting, bowling, fielding, and more.

Batting is one of the key skills in cricket, and it's like trying to hit a bullseye with a banana peel. Players need to develop hand-eye coordination, timing, and shot selection. It's like participating in a comedy show, where they have to deliver the perfect punchline (shot) to make the audience (spectators) burst into laughter (applause). Batting practice involves honing techniques, improving footwork, and mastering different strokes. And just like in a comedy routine, a good sense of timing and improvisation can make all the difference.

Bowling is another crucial skill, and it's like trying to pull off a magic trick with a cricket ball. Players need to develop speed, accuracy, and variations to deceive the batsmen. It's like a magician performing tricks, where the element of surprise and misdirection plays a crucial role. Bowling practice involves perfecting the run-up, release point, and mastering different types of deliveries. And just like in a magic show, a cleverly executed delivery can leave the batsman and the audience wondering what just happened.

Fielding is often considered the unsung hero of cricket, and it's like being a circus performer juggling multiple objects. Players need agility, reflexes, and anticipation to save runs and take spectacular catches. It's like a circus act, where the fielder has to jump, dive, and make acrobatic movements to showcase their skills. Fielding practice involves drills to improve catching, throwing, and agility. And just like in a circus, a remarkable fielding display can leave the crowd in awe and bring a touch of humor to the game.

Wicketkeeping is a specialized skill in cricket, and it's like being a professional plate spinner in a circus. Wicketkeepers need lightning-fast reflexes, sharp eyesight, and good anticipation to react to the bowler's deliveries. It's like keeping multiple plates spinning in the air without letting any of them fall. Wicketkeeping practice involves developing agility, hand-eye coordination, and practicing the art of stumping and catching. And just like in a circus act, a wicketkeeper's quick reactions and nimble movements can provide moments of entertainment and laughter.

Physical fitness is essential for cricket, and it's like maintaining a healthy diet while constantly craving for a slice of pizza. Players need to develop strength, endurance, and flexibility to excel in the game. It's like trying to balance a healthy lifestyle while indulging in occasional treats. Fitness training involves a combination of cardio, strength exercises, and agility drills. And just like in a healthy eating plan, the occasional cheat day (treating oneself to a guilty pleasure) can keep the spirits high.

In conclusion, cricket skills development is a journey that requires dedication, practice, and a touch of humor. Players work hard to master the art of batting, bowling, fielding, and wicketkeeping. It's like being part of a comedy routine, where timing, improvisation, and a good sense of humor can make the game more enjoyable. So, the next time you watch a cricket match, appreciate the skills on display and the countless hours of practice that go into developing those skills. And who knows, you might even find inspiration to add a little humor to your own skill development journey, be it on the cricket field or in any other aspect of life.

Batting drills and exercises

Batting in cricket requires finesse, technique, and a dash of humor to navigate through the challenges. To develop these skills, players engage in various drills and exercises that are as diverse and entertaining as a comedy skit. Let's explore some of the batting drills and exercises that help players improve their technique and timing while adding a touch of humor to the mix.

The "Banana Peel" Drill: This drill focuses on footwork and balance, much like trying to stay upright after stepping on a banana peel. Players practice quick and precise foot movements while maintaining stability. The goal is to avoid slipping and falling, just like a comic character in a slapstick comedy.

The "Dancing Feet" Drill: Batting requires nimble footwork, and this drill resembles a dance routine. Players practice moving their feet swiftly and gracefully, as if performing on a dance floor. It's all about finding the right rhythm and coordinating foot movements with the delivery of the ball.

The "Mirror, Mirror" Drill: This drill involves practicing shots while facing a mirror. Players can observe their technique and make adjustments, just like actors rehearsing their lines in front of a mirror. It's an opportunity to perfect their strokes and ensure they are picture-perfect.

The "Comedy Sketch" Drill: In this drill, players simulate different game scenarios and adapt their shot selection accordingly. It's like improvising lines in a comedy sketch, where they have to think on their feet and choose the most suitable shot to deliver the punchline. This drill helps players develop decision-making skills and adaptability.

The "Timing is Everything" Drill: Batting is all about timing, much like delivering a perfectly-timed punchline in a joke. In this drill, players focus on getting the timing right by practicing hitting the ball at the precise moment. It's like delivering a comedic punchline with impeccable timing to generate laughter from the audience.

The "Catch Me if You Can" Drill: This drill adds an element of fun and competitiveness to batting practice. Players challenge each other to hit the ball in such a way that it becomes difficult for fielders to catch. It's like playing a game of tag, where the batsman tries to evade the fielders' grasp with well-placed shots.

The "Switch-Hit Surprise" Drill: This drill involves practicing the switch-hit, a shot where the batsman changes their stance and hand position to surprise the bowler. It's like a magician pulling off a surprising trick that leaves the audience in awe. Players work on perfecting this unorthodox shot, adding a touch of unpredictability to their batting repertoire.

The "One-Handed Wonder" Drill: This drill focuses on developing hand-eye coordination and quick reactions. Players practice batting with only one hand, challenging themselves to maintain control and play shots with precision. It's like performing a juggling act, where they have to keep the ball in play using just one hand.

In conclusion, batting drills and exercises in cricket are not only essential for improving technique and timing but also provide a dose of humor and entertainment. These drills add a touch of creativity and playfulness to the practice sessions, making the learning process enjoyable. So, the next time you see a batsman play a magnificent shot, remember the behind-the-scenes work that goes into perfecting those skills, often accompanied by laughter and a few comedic moments.

Bowling drills and exercises

Bowling in cricket requires skill, precision, and a touch of humor to keep the game interesting. Players engage in various drills and exercises to improve their bowling technique and develop the finesse required to bamboozle the batsmen. Let's explore some of the bowling drills and exercises that add a dash of humor to the cricketing mix.

The "Dancing Shoes" Drill: This drill focuses on footwork and agility, much like a lively dance routine. Players practice quick and nimble foot movements, resembling dancers gliding across the floor. The goal is to maintain balance and coordination, just like a dancer performing an intricate routine.

The "Hula Hoop" Drill: This drill aims to improve accuracy and precision. Bowlers place hula hoops on the pitch, and the objective is to bowl the ball through the hoop. It's like trying to throw a ring around a target at a carnival, adding a fun and light-hearted element to the practice session.

The "Magic Hat" Drill: In this drill, bowlers focus on mastering variations and deceptive deliveries. It's like a magician pulling tricks out of a hat, leaving the batsman wondering what's coming next. Bowlers practice spinning the ball, bowling slower balls, or perfecting their yorkers, adding an element of surprise to their repertoire.

The "Human Wicket" Drill: This drill involves setting up a mock wicket with a player standing as the "stump." Bowlers aim to knock the "stump" over with their deliveries, much like knocking down pins in a bowling alley. It's a lighthearted way to work on accuracy and targeting specific areas.

The "Race Against Time" Drill: Bowlers challenge themselves to complete an over within a specified time limit. It's like a race against the clock, where they have to maintain accuracy and pace while keeping the game flowing. This drill helps improve bowling efficiency and develops the ability to handle pressure.

The "Double Trouble" Drill: Bowlers practice bowling consecutive deliveries at different lengths and speeds. It's like a double act, where they switch between different variations to keep the batsman guessing. This drill hones their ability to mix up their deliveries and maintain control.

The "Evasive Action" Drill: Bowlers simulate game situations where they have to bowl to a batsman attempting big shots. The objective is to bowl accurately while avoiding being hit for boundaries. It's like a game of cat and mouse, where bowlers try to outsmart the batsman with well-placed deliveries.

The "Invisible Hurdle" Drill: This drill focuses on developing a smooth and fluid bowling action. Bowlers practice their run-up and delivery stride while imagining an invisible hurdle they must clear. It's like an athlete gracefully leaping over hurdles, ensuring a seamless and effortless bowling action.

In conclusion, bowling drills and exercises in cricket not only help players improve their technique and precision but also add a touch of humor and creativity to the practice sessions. These drills create a playful atmosphere, making the learning process enjoyable while honing the necessary skills. So, the next time you witness a bowler bamboozling the batsman with a magical delivery, remember the behind-the-scenes work that goes into perfecting those skills, often accompanied by laughter and a few amusing moments.

Fielding drills and exercises

Fielding in cricket requires agility, reflexes, and a good sense of humor to make those diving catches and acrobatic saves. Players engage in various drills and exercises to improve their fielding skills and develop the finesse required to become exceptional fielders. Let's explore some of the fielding drills and exercises that add a touch of humor to the cricketing mix.

The "Hot Potato" Drill: This drill focuses on quick reactions and reflexes. Players form a circle and pass a ball rapidly to each other, resembling a game of hot potato. The objective is to catch and release the ball swiftly, keeping the momentum going while dodging imaginary "hot potatoes."

The "Dive and Roll" Drill: This drill helps players practice their diving and rolling techniques. They simulate fielding situations where they have to dive to save boundaries and then quickly recover by rolling back onto their feet. It's like a graceful dance move combined with the skill of a contortionist.

The "Crazy Catches" Drill: This drill adds an element of unpredictability to fielding practice. Coaches or fellow players throw the ball in unexpected directions, challenging fielders to adjust quickly and make unconventional catches. It's like a game of catch with a twist, keeping fielders on their toes and testing their reflexes.

The "Human Wall" Drill: This drill involves fielders forming a line, closely spaced, and attempting to stop the ball from passing through. It's like creating a human wall to prevent the ball from sneaking past. Fielders work together, using their bodies and quick reflexes to block the ball and protect the boundary.

The "Bullseye" Drill: In this drill, fielders aim to hit a specific target with their throws. Whether it's knocking down a set of stumps or hitting a target on a wall, it's like playing a game of darts on the cricket field. This drill improves accuracy and throwing technique while adding a fun competitive element.

The "Switcheroo" Drill: Fielders practice quick transitions and exchanges while moving between positions. It's like a game of musical chairs, where fielders have to switch places seamlessly based on the bowler's line and length. This drill enhances communication and teamwork among fielders.

The "Distractor" Drill: Fielders practice maintaining focus and concentration amidst distractions. Coaches or teammates create noise or movement to divert their attention while they attempt to catch the ball. It's like a circus act, testing fielders' ability to ignore the chaos around them and stay focused on the task at hand.

The "Superman" Drill: This drill involves fielders diving and stretching to take high catches or reach for balls near the boundary. It's like emulating the iconic superhero with gravity-defying leaps and incredible catches. Fielders push their limits, aiming to fly like Superman and take stunning catches.

In conclusion, fielding drills and exercises in cricket not only help players improve their reflexes, agility, and throwing accuracy but also add a touch of humor and creativity to the practice sessions. These drills create an enjoyable atmosphere, where players can showcase their athleticism and have fun while honing their fielding skills. So, the next time you witness a fielder making an unbelievable catch or executing a lightning-fast run-out, remember the behind-the-scenes work that goes into developing those skills, often accompanied by laughter and a few amusing moments.

Fitness and conditioning for cricket

Fitness and conditioning play a vital role in cricket, where players need to be agile, strong, and have the endurance to perform at their best. While it may seem like all fun and games on the cricket field, the truth is that behind those spectacular shots and thunderous throws, there lies a lot of hard work and fitness training. Let's explore some interesting and effective fitness and conditioning techniques that cricketers employ, with a dash of humor.

"Catch Me If You Can" Cardio: Cricket matches can last for hours, and players need the stamina to keep up with the demands of the game. To build endurance, cricketers engage in cardio exercises like running, cycling, or swimming. They playfully imagine themselves being chased by an opposing team member, motivating them to run faster and farther.

"Strong as a Bull" Strength Training: Cricketers need both upper and lower body strength to deliver powerful shots and bowl with accuracy. They hit the gym, lifting weights and doing exercises like squats, lunges, and bench presses. Sometimes, they even imagine themselves as strong as a bull, ready to charge the field with all their might.

"Flexibility is Key" Stretching: Flexibility is crucial in cricket, allowing players to reach for those high catches or execute agile movements. They incorporate stretching exercises into their routines, like yoga or dynamic stretches. Picture cricketers twisting and bending like contortionists, gracefully stretching their bodies like elastic bands.

"The Balancing Act" Core Training: A strong core is essential for stability and balance in cricket. Cricketers perform exercises such as planks, Russian twists, and medicine ball exercises to strengthen their core muscles. They often joke about their core being as solid as a rock, allowing them to maintain their balance while dodging bouncers or executing nimble footwork.

"The Speedster" Speed and Agility Training: Quick movements on the field are crucial in cricket, whether it's sprinting between the wickets or chasing down a ball. Cricketers engage in speed and agility drills, like shuttle runs, ladder drills, and cone exercises. They imagine themselves as speedy superheroes, racing against time to save the day.

"The Power Pose" Plyometric Training: Explosive power is needed in cricket for big shots and fast bowling. Cricketers incorporate plyometric exercises like box jumps, burpees, and medicine ball throws into their training. They strike power poses, imagining themselves as superheroes ready to unleash their strength and conquer the field.

"Catch a Break" Recovery Techniques: Recovery is just as important as training itself. Cricketers use various techniques like ice baths, foam rolling, and massage therapy to aid muscle recovery and prevent injuries. They humorously refer to these recovery sessions as "catching a break" from the grueling training regime.

"Mind over Matter" Mental Training: Cricket is as much a mental game as it is physical. Cricketers practice meditation, visualization, and mindfulness techniques to stay focused and maintain a positive mindset. They often joke about having a "Zen mode" or "cricket Zen" to keep their minds sharp and agile.

In conclusion, fitness and conditioning are vital components of cricket, and cricketers employ various techniques with a touch of humor to keep themselves motivated and engaged. The blend of hard work and lightheartedness creates an enjoyable training atmosphere, where players can push their boundaries and strive for excellence. So, the next time you see a cricketer executing a powerful shot or making a lightning-fast run, remember the fitness and conditioning journey behind those moments, filled with dedication, laughter, and a few humorous anecdotes.

Umpiring and Officiating in Cricket

Umpiring and officiating in cricket may seem like a thankless job, but it's an integral part of the game. While players battle it out on the field, umpires ensure fair play, make critical decisions, and keep the game running smoothly. Let's dive into the world of umpiring in cricket, with a sprinkle of humor along the way.

"The Eye in the Sky" Umpire's Role: Umpires serve as the guardians of the game, enforcing the laws, and making crucial decisions. They are responsible for judging whether a batsman is out or safe, determining the legality of deliveries, and overseeing fair play. In a way, they are like the all-seeing eyes in the sky, with the power to make or break a player's day.

"Signals and Gestures" Umpire Language: Umpires communicate with players, officials, and spectators through a unique language of signals and gestures. From signaling boundaries with outstretched arms to raising that dreaded finger for an out decision, these gestures are like a secret code that only cricket enthusiasts can decipher. Sometimes, even the players have a hard time understanding these "umpire handshakes."

"The Art of Balance" Umpire Positioning: Umpires must position themselves strategically to get the best view of the action. They often find themselves dancing a delicate balancing act, moving swiftly to be in the right position to make accurate judgments. It's like they have their own version of a carefully choreographed dance routine.

"Technology to the Rescue" Umpire Decision Review System (DRS): In recent years, technology has become a valuable tool in umpiring. The Decision Review System (DRS) allows teams to challenge umpire decisions using video replays and ball-tracking technology. It's like umpires now have a tech-savvy assistant to help them make those difficult decisions. However, even with technology, controversies and debates can still arise, reminding us that cricket is a game of uncertainties.

"The Unseen Heroes" Third Umpires and Match Referees: Alongside the on-field umpires, there are third umpires and match referees who play crucial roles behind the scenes. Third umpires review close decisions using multiple camera angles and communicate with the on-field umpires through radio communication. Match referees, on the other hand, oversee the conduct of the game, ensuring fair play and maintaining discipline. They are like the unsung heroes of the cricket world, working diligently to uphold the spirit of the game.

"Umpire Banter" Player-Umpire Interactions: Player-umpire interactions can sometimes be quite entertaining. Captains and players engage in lively discussions and debates, trying to convince the umpires of their viewpoint. It's like a comedic duel of words, with each side trying to outwit the other. But at the end of the day, it's the umpire's decision that stands.

"The Umpire's Verdict" Controversial Decisions: Umpires sometimes find themselves at the center of controversy due to contentious decisions. These moments spark intense debates among players, pundits, and fans, fueling endless discussions over cups of tea. But hey, controversy is part of the game, and it keeps everyone on their toes.

In conclusion, umpires and officiating in cricket are indispensable to maintaining fair play and ensuring the smooth running of the game. Umpires juggle their roles with precision and make critical decisions that shape the outcome of matches. Their unique gestures, positioning, and interaction with players add color to the cricketing experience. So, the next time you watch a cricket match, spare a thought for those brave souls in white, doing their best to keep the game fair and entertaining, all while providing us with some unforgettable moments and a few laughs along the way.

Cricket umpiring rules and requirements

Cricket umpiring is no ordinary job. It requires a deep understanding of the game, a sharp eye, and nerves of steel. Let's delve into the rules and requirements of cricket umpiring, with a touch of humor to lighten the mood.

"The Rule Book: A Umpire's Best Friend": Umpires must be well-versed in the laws of cricket. The rule book becomes their trusty sidekick, like a superhero's cape that guides them through the complexities of the game. It's their job to interpret and enforce these laws with precision, even if it feels like deciphering ancient hieroglyphics at times.

"No Glasses, No Problem": Umpires need to have exceptional vision to make accurate decisions. However, for those with less-than-perfect eyesight, fear not! Umpires can rely on technology, like the big screens and zoomed-in replays, to aid their vision. After all, even superheroes need a little help from time to time.

"Umpire Signals: A Game of Charades": Umpires communicate their decisions using a variety of signals, like a secret language that only they and the players understand. From raising a finger for an out decision to extending arms for a boundary, it's like playing an elaborate game of charades. Sometimes, even the players join in the fun, attempting to imitate the umpire signals during friendly banter.

"The Power of the Umpire's Voice": Umpires must have a strong and authoritative voice to command the respect of the players. It's like having a vocal superpower that can silence even the most boisterous of crowds. So, umpires, remember to channel your inner superhero and make sure your voice carries across the field.

"Keeping Up with the Pace": Cricket matches can be fast-paced, and umpires need to keep up with the action. They must be agile and nimble on their feet, moving swiftly to get into position for the best view. It's like a dance routine where the umpires twirl and spin to ensure they don't miss a single moment.

"Patience: The Umpire's Virtue": Umpires must possess extraordinary patience, especially during long and intense matches. They must remain calm and composed, even in the face of heated debates and arguments. It's like practicing the art of Zen amidst the chaos of a cricket ground.

"The Umpire's Secret Weapon: Confidence": Umpires must exude confidence in their decisions, even if they're unsure at times. It's like wearing an invisible suit of armor that shields them from doubts and second-guessing. Confidence is their superpower, helping them make split-second judgments without hesitation.

"Qualifications and Training: More than Just a Love for Cricket": Becoming a cricket umpire requires more than just a passion for the game. Umpires need to undergo training programs and obtain certifications to hone their skills. It's like attending a secret academy where they learn the art of umpiring and embrace their inner superhero.

In conclusion, cricket umpiring is a unique blend of knowledge, skill, and nerves of steel. Umpires must be well-versed in the laws of the game, possess sharp vision, and maintain a calm and confident demeanor. It's a role that demands agility, patience, and the ability to make split-second decisions. So, the next time you watch a cricket match, take a moment to appreciate the umpires who ensure fair play and keep the game running smoothly. They are the unsung heroes of the cricketing world, donning their invisible capes and making their mark with every decision.

Types of cricket umpires

In the world of cricket, there are different types of umpires who play crucial roles in ensuring fair play and upholding the laws of the game. Let's explore these types of cricket umpires with a touch of humor to lighten the mood.

"On-Field Umpires: The Guardians of Fair Play": These are the umpires you see standing on the field, making decisions in real-time. They are like the superheroes of the cricketing world, donning their uniforms and armed with their trusty rule book. Their job is to make judgments on appeals, determine boundaries, and keep a watchful eye on the proceedings. It's like being the sheriff in a wild west showdown, ensuring justice prevails.

"TV Umpires: The Super Sleuths": TV umpires, also known as third umpires, have a special role in reviewing decisions using technology. They watch the game from multiple camera angles, like detectives analyzing a crime scene. Their mission is to assist on-field umpires in making accurate decisions on controversial or close calls. They provide a valuable second opinion and use slow-motion replays to solve the mysteries of the cricketing universe.

"Match Referees: The Voice of Reason": Match referees act as the custodians of the game's spirit and conduct. They oversee the behavior of players, captains, and the overall conduct of the match. They have the power to impose penalties and maintain discipline on and off the field. Think of them as the wise judges who bring order to the chaos and ensure fair play prevails.

"Fourth Umpires: The Handy Helpers": Fourth umpires are like the utility players of the umpiring world. They assist the on-field umpires by carrying messages, providing new balls, and managing substitutes. They are the unsung heroes who ensure the smooth running of the game behind the scenes. It's like having a trusty sidekick who anticipates the umpire's needs and saves the day.

"Umpire Coaches: The Gurus of Umpiring": Umpire coaches play a vital role in developing and mentoring umpires at various levels. They provide guidance, training, and feedback to aspiring umpires, helping them refine their skills and knowledge. They are like the wise sages who pass on their wisdom and ensure a new generation of umpires are ready to take on the challenges of the game.

"Neutral Umpires: The Global Envoys": In international cricket, neutral umpires are appointed to ensure impartiality and eliminate any bias. They are like ambassadors, representing the spirit of fair play across different nations. It's like having a united coalition of umpires who bring different perspectives and foster a sense of camaraderie on the field.

Each type of cricket umpire plays a unique role in the game, contributing to its integrity and smooth functioning. They are the guardians of fair play, the super sleuths who solve mysteries, the voice of reason, the handy helpers, the gurus of umpiring, and the global envoys of impartiality.

Next time you watch a cricket match, take a moment to appreciate the efforts of these umpires who work tirelessly behind the scenes. They ensure that the game is played within the spirit of cricket and that justice is served. They are the unsung heroes, embracing their roles with a blend of expertise, integrity, and a touch of humor. So, let's raise a toast to the umpires who keep the game alive and thriving, adding their unique flavor to the world of cricket.

Scorekeeping and officiating duties

Scorekeeping and officiating duties in cricket are often overlooked but play a vital role in the smooth running of the game. Let's delve into the world of scorekeepers and officials with a touch of humor.

"Scorekeepers: The Cricket Accountants": Scorekeepers are the unsung heroes of the game, diligently recording every run, wicket, and ball. They are like accountants meticulously balancing the cricketing ledger. Armed with their trusty scorebooks and pens, they decode the complex language of cricket into neat columns and figures. It's like solving a mathematical puzzle while being entertained by the cricketing drama.

"Match Managers: The Conductors of Cricket": Match managers, also known as scorers, are responsible for maintaining the official scorecard. They ensure that the score is accurately updated, capture player statistics, and communicate with the umpires and players. They are like conductors, orchestrating the symphony of cricket, keeping everyone in sync and ensuring a smooth flow of information.

"Timekeepers: The Masters of Time": Timekeepers play a critical role in keeping the game on schedule. They ensure that the match adheres to the allocated timeframes, reminding players, umpires, and officials about the time constraints. It's like being the time lords of cricket, juggling the hours and minutes to maintain the rhythm of the game.

"Match Announcers: The Voice of the Stadium": Match announcers entertain the crowd and provide important updates during the game. They describe the action, announce players' names, and keep the audience engaged. With their charismatic voices, they add a touch of drama and excitement to the proceedings. It's like being the DJs of cricket, setting the atmosphere and getting the crowd on their feet.

"Ground Staff: The Magicians of Maintenance": Ground staff, though not directly involved in officiating, are responsible for preparing and maintaining the playing surface. They ensure the pitch is in optimal condition, the boundaries are marked, and the outfield is well-manicured. They are like the magicians behind the scenes, conjuring a field that is both pleasing to the eye and conducive to thrilling cricketing encounters.

"Technology Officials: The Wizards of Innovation": In modern cricket, technology officials handle innovations such as ball-tracking systems, Hawkeye, and Snicko. They assist umpires and officials in making decisions by analyzing various technological aids. They are like wizards, using technology to unravel the mysteries of the game and bring clarity to complex situations.

Each of these roles contributes to the smooth functioning and enjoyment of the game. From scorekeepers maintaining the records to timekeepers keeping the game on schedule, from match announcers entertaining the crowd to ground staff preparing the perfect field, and from technology officials harnessing technology to umpires ensuring fair play, every individual plays a crucial part in the cricketing ecosystem.

So, the next time you watch a cricket match, spare a thought for these behind-the-scenes heroes. They may not grab the headlines or receive the spotlight, but their contributions are invaluable. They bring order to the chaos, record the achievements, and ensure that the game we love continues to thrive.

Let's raise our imaginary hats to the scorekeepers, match managers, timekeepers, match announcers, ground staff, and technology officials who add their own touch of magic to the sport of cricket. Their dedication, attention to detail, and sense of humor make the cricketing experience even more enjoyable for players and fans alike.

Coaching and Training in Cricket

Coaching and training in cricket are the pillars of success for players and teams. Let's explore this world of cricket coaching with a dash of humor.

"Coaches: The Cricket Gurus": Cricket coaches are like the gurus of the game, imparting their wisdom and knowledge to aspiring cricketers. They analyze players' techniques, strategize game plans, and provide valuable guidance. They are a blend of teachers, motivators, and psychologists, helping players navigate the ups and downs of the sport. Think of them as Yoda with a cricket bat!

"Net Sessions: The Battle of Bat and Ball": Net sessions are the battlegrounds where players sharpen their skills. It's like a fierce duel between bat and ball, where bowlers aim to outfox the batsmen, and batsmen strive to score runs. Amidst the sounds of cracking willows and thudding balls, players refine their techniques and develop their shot repertoire. It's a testing ground where talent meets determination.

"Fitness Training: Building the Cricketing Machines": Fitness training is an essential part of cricket, ensuring players have the stamina, agility, and strength to excel on the field. From grueling gym sessions to intense cardio workouts, players transform into finely-tuned cricketing machines. They endure the pain to gain the competitive edge, all in the pursuit of glory. It's like a superhero training montage, but with cricket pads and helmets.

"Fielding Drills: Acrobatics on the Cricket Field": Fielding drills are the acrobatic displays of athleticism on the cricket field. Players dive, leap, and stretch to stop the ball and take breathtaking catches. It's like a circus act, where fielders become the daredevils, defying gravity to save runs. They showcase their agility and flexibility, leaving the crowd in awe.

"Mental Preparation: The Battle within": Cricket is not just a physical game; it's a mental battle too. Coaches work on players' mental preparation, teaching them to stay focused, handle pressure, and maintain a positive mindset. They instill mental resilience and teach players to overcome obstacles with a smile. It's like a Jedi training camp, equipping players with the mental strength to conquer any challenge.

"Video Analysis: The Cricket Detective Agency": Video analysis has revolutionized cricket coaching. Coaches dissect every aspect of a player's performance, studying their technique, footwork, and decision-making. It's like being part of a cricket detective agency, where every movement is scrutinized, and weaknesses are identified. Armed with this knowledge, players can fine-tune their skills and improve their game.

Cricket coaching and training are not just about honing skills; they are about instilling values like discipline, teamwork, and perseverance. Coaches play a pivotal role in shaping not only players' cricketing abilities but also their characters.

So, the next time you witness a stunning catch or a perfectly executed cover drive, remember the coaches and trainers who have contributed to that moment. Their expertise, guidance, and sometimes hilarious anecdotes make the journey of cricket even more memorable.

Let's celebrate the coaches, the training sessions, the grueling fitness routines, and the mental battles. They all contribute to the magic of cricket, where players strive for excellence and fans experience moments of pure joy.

In the end, cricket coaching and training are not just about winning matches; they are about nurturing a love for the game and instilling a lifelong passion. Whether it's in the nets, on the field, or in the minds of players, the impact of coaching and training reverberates throughout the cricketing world.

Coaching techniques and methods

Coaching techniques and methods in cricket are as diverse as the array of shots played on the field. Let's delve into this world of coaching with a touch of humor.

"The Chameleon Coach": Cricket coaches are like chameleons, adapting their coaching style to each player's unique needs. They tailor their methods to bring out the best in each individual. Whether it's correcting a batting stance or fine-tuning a bowling action, they possess the ability to blend in with the player's strengths and weaknesses.

"The Power of Visualization": Coaches often employ visualization techniques to help players mentally prepare for the game. They encourage players to imagine themselves executing perfect shots or bowling deadly deliveries. It's like a cricketing daydream where players envision themselves hitting sixes and taking wickets, boosting their confidence and belief.

"Drills with a Twist": Coaches use a variety of drills to enhance skills, but they also know how to inject some fun into the training sessions. From relay races with cricket bats to blindfolded catching challenges, they spice up the drills to keep players engaged and motivated. It's like a carnival of cricket where players enjoy the process while honing their skills.

"The Art of Communication": Effective communication is key to successful coaching. Coaches use a mix of technical jargon, hand gestures, and animated facial expressions to convey their instructions. They are like cricketing mimes, painting vivid pictures with their words and gestures, ensuring players understand and execute the desired techniques.

"The Motivational Magicians": Coaches are master motivators, knowing just the right words to inspire players. They give pep talks that ignite the fire within, reminding players of their potential and the importance of teamwork. It's like a magical spell that transforms self-doubt into self-belief, motivating players to give their all on the field.

"Data-driven Coaching": In the age of technology, coaches use data analysis tools to dissect players' performances. They pore over statistics and graphs like cricketing statisticians, identifying patterns and areas for improvement. Armed with this data, they can provide precise feedback and tailor training programs for optimal results.

"The Tactical Wizards": Coaches are tactical wizards, devising game plans to outsmart the opposition. They strategize like chess grandmasters, analyzing the strengths and weaknesses of the opposition and adjusting field placements and bowling tactics accordingly. It's like a game of cricket chess, where every move is carefully calculated to gain the upper hand.

Coaching techniques and methods in cricket are a blend of science, psychology, and intuition. Coaches play a crucial role in nurturing talent, instilling discipline, and fostering a love for the game.

So, the next time you witness a beautifully executed cover drive or a perfectly bowled yorker, spare a thought for the coaches behind the scenes. Their techniques, methods, and occasional moments of comic relief contribute to the development of skilled cricketers and memorable moments on the field.

Let's appreciate the chameleon-like abilities of coaches, their creativity in designing drills, and their motivational prowess. They are the guiding lights who shape the future of cricket, one player at a time.

In the end, coaching techniques and methods are not just about winning matches; they are about building character, fostering camaraderie, and instilling a lifelong passion for the game. Whether it's in the nets, on the field, or in the minds of players, the impact of coaching reverberates throughout the cricketing world.

Player development and progress

Player development and progress in cricket is like watching a caterpillar transform into a graceful butterfly, albeit with a bat and ball. Let's explore this journey of growth and improvement with a touch of humor.

"From Grasshoppers to Giants": Just like insects, cricket players start small. They learn the basics of batting, bowling, and fielding, resembling grasshoppers hopping around the field. But with dedication and practice, they evolve into giants of the game, smashing boundaries and taking wickets with finesse.

"The Spider-Web of Skills": Cricket is a sport that requires a multitude of skills. Players must master the art of timing, footwork, hand-eye coordination, and tactical awareness. It's like a complex spider-web, with each skill interconnected and essential for success. As players develop and refine these skills, their performance on the field becomes a masterful dance.

"Coaches: the Fairy Godparents": Coaches play a vital role in player development, acting as fairy godparents in the cricketing world. They guide players through the ups and downs, offering wisdom, support, and occasional magical interventions. With their guidance, players blossom and discover their true potential, just like Cinderella at the ball.

"Milestones: More Than Just Numbers": Player development is marked by milestones, but they represent more than just numbers. Scoring a century or taking a five-wicket haul is an achievement that reflects hard work, determination, and skill. These milestones are like badges of honor, showcasing a player's progress and earning them respect in the cricketing fraternity.

"Failures: Stepping Stones to Success": In cricket, failures are inevitable, but they serve as stepping stones to success. Every dropped catch, missed run, or dismissed wicket teaches players valuable lessons. It's like tripping and falling on the way to the prize, only to rise stronger and more resilient. Embracing failures is an integral part of the player development journey.

"The Role of Experience": Experience is the secret sauce that enhances player development. As players gain exposure to different conditions, opponents, and formats of the game, they become seasoned campaigners. It's like a seasoning that adds flavor and depth to their cricketing skills. The more experience they accumulate, the better equipped they are to handle various challenges.

"The Joy of Progress": Perhaps the most rewarding aspect of player development is witnessing personal growth. From mastering a new shot to bowling a perfect yorker, players experience moments of sheer joy as they see their skills improve. It's like a child discovering the joy of riding a bicycle without training wheels, a testament to their hard work paying off.

Player development and progress in cricket is a dynamic and ongoing process. It requires dedication, perseverance, and a healthy dose of humor to navigate the highs and lows of the game.

So, whether you're a budding cricketer or a passionate fan, remember that every player's journey is unique. Enjoy the process, embrace the challenges, and savor the moments of progress. And above all, keep a sense of humor handy to laugh at the occasional missteps along the way.

In the end, player development is not just about becoming a better cricketer; it's about personal growth, building character, and forging lifelong friendships. It's a journey that transforms individuals, leaving an indelible mark on their lives and the cricketing world.

Building successful cricket teams

Building a successful cricket team is no different from assembling a diverse group of superheroes to save the world. Let's explore the key elements required to create a winning team with a touch of humor.

"The Avengers of Cricket": A successful cricket team is like a group of superheroes with complementary skills and abilities. Just as Iron Man has his suit, Captain America his shield, and Thor his hammer, each player brings unique strengths to the team. From explosive batsmen to crafty spinners and lightning-fast fielders, the team is a mix of diverse talents.

"The Selection Conundrum": Selecting the right players for the team is akin to solving a complex puzzle. The captain and selectors analyze players' performances, form, and fitness, trying to find the perfect fit. It's like assembling a team of puzzle pieces, ensuring they fit together seamlessly to create a winning picture.

"Team Chemistry: The X-Factor": Like the Avengers, cricket teams need strong chemistry to succeed. Players must bond, trust, and communicate effectively both on and off the field. It's like the chemistry between Thor and Hulk – a powerful combination that can smash any challenge that comes their way.

"Captaincy: The Superpower": The captain is the team's leader, the superhero who guides them through thick and thin. With tactical acumen and the ability to make tough decisions, the captain is like Doctor Strange, foreseeing the game's twists and turns. Their leadership can turn the tide of a match, just as Iron Man's leadership drives the Avengers to victory.

"Practice Makes Superheroes": Superheroes hone their skills through rigorous training, and cricket teams are no different. Hours of practice, drills, and simulations are like the training sessions at the Avengers' headquarters. It's where players sharpen their abilities, learn new strategies, and develop the muscle memory needed for game-changing performances.

"The Role of Support Staff": Behind every superhero team, there is a team of support staff providing crucial assistance. Coaches, physiotherapists, and analysts are like the unsung heroes behind the scenes. They provide guidance, help with recovery, and analyze opponents, ensuring the team is well-prepared for battle.

"Embracing Unity and Diversity": Successful teams embrace unity while celebrating diversity. Just as the Avengers come from different backgrounds and have varied personalities, cricket teams consist of players from diverse cultures and regions. Embracing and respecting these differences create a stronger bond and contribute to the team's success.

"Team Spirit: Assemble!" The team spirit is the glue that holds everything together. Like the rallying cry of the Avengers, cricket teams must unite under a common purpose and support each other through the ups and downs. It's the spirit that fuels comebacks, inspires remarkable performances, and makes the team greater than the sum of its parts.

Building a successful cricket team requires more than individual talent. It demands a collective effort, a shared vision, and a sprinkle of humor along the way. So, let's enjoy the journey, cheer for our favorite teams, and celebrate the superhero-like performances that cricket has to offer. Together, we can witness the birth of legendary teams that will be remembered for generations to come.

Watching Cricket: TV and Live Events

Watching cricket is like being part of an epic adventure unfolding right before your eyes. Whether you're glued to your television or lucky enough to witness a live event, the experience is nothing short of exhilarating. Let's dive into the world of cricket viewing, with a touch of humor along the way.

"Cricket Fever: A Highly Contagious Condition": Watching cricket is not just a pastime; it's a contagious condition that sweeps through fans worldwide. Once infected, you become a lifelong enthusiast, eagerly awaiting every match as if it were the climax of a gripping blockbuster movie.

"The Comfort of Your Couch": Watching cricket from the comfort of your own home is like having the best seat in the stadium. You can lounge on your couch, indulge in snacks, and even wear your lucky pajamas – all without worrying about the infamous stadium queues or unpredictable weather.

"Commentators: The Voice of Cricket": Commentators are the unsung heroes of cricket viewing. With their wit, expert analysis, and colorful descriptions, they bring the game to life. Their banter and catchphrases are like the secret sauce that adds flavor to the cricket-watching experience.

"Crazy Fan Antics": Cricket fans are known for their eccentric antics during matches. From painting their faces in team colors to wearing outrageous costumes, they add a vibrant atmosphere to the game. Spotting a fan dressed as a superhero or dancing in the stands is as common as a wicket falling.

"The Nail-Biting Suspense": Cricket matches are a roller coaster of emotions. The tension builds with every ball, and the suspense can make your heart skip a beat. It's like watching a thriller movie with unexpected plot twists and dramatic moments that leave you on the edge of your seat.

"The Big Screens and Spectacular Stadiums": Attending a live cricket match is an unforgettable experience. The buzz of the crowd, the roar of excitement, and the awe-inspiring stadiums create an electric atmosphere. The giant screens display close-ups of players and replays, ensuring you don't miss a single moment.

"The Socializing Bonanza": Watching cricket is not just about the game; it's a social event where friends and family come together. Whether it's gathering around the TV or joining the crowd at a stadium, it's an opportunity to bond, cheer, and share in the joy (and occasional heartbreak) of the game.

"The Memorable Moments": Cricket matches produce moments that etch themselves into the annals of history. Whether it's a breathtaking catch, a blistering century, or an unexpected victory, these moments become legends and are replayed for years to come. They are the highlights that fans discuss and relive with fondness.

"The Art of Channel Surfing": Cricket matches can last for hours, and sometimes you need a break from the tension. That's when channel surfing becomes an art form. You can catch up on other shows, check the news, or even squeeze in a quick power nap – all while keeping one eye on the game.

"The Community of Fans": Cricket brings together a global community of passionate fans. From friendly banter on social media to heated debates at the local pub, being a cricket fan means joining a community that transcends borders and unites people from all walks of life.

Watching cricket is not just about the sport itself; it's about the camaraderie, the thrill, and the shared love for the game. So, grab your snacks, find your favorite spot, and immerse yourself in the world of cricket – where every match is an adventure waiting to unfold.

How to watch cricket on TV

If you're a cricket fan, you know that watching the game on TV is a cherished pastime. It's like having a front-row seat to all the action, drama, and excitement. To ensure you make the most of your cricket viewing experience, here are some humorous yet practical tips on how to watch cricket on TV:

"Claim the Remote Control": Before the match starts, make sure you secure control of the TV remote. This is a critical step to ensure uninterrupted cricket viewing. Be prepared to defend it with all your might, employing strategic hiding spots and well-timed bathroom breaks.

"Snacks: Fuel for the Cricket Marathon": Watching cricket is a marathon, not a sprint. Stock up on snacks and beverages that will sustain you throughout the match. Whether it's the classic popcorn, a bowl of nachos, or a plate of samosas, make sure you have a tasty arsenal at your disposal.

"Master the Art of Multitasking": Cricket matches can last for hours, and it's essential to master the art of multitasking. Use commercial breaks to quickly attend to life's necessities – make a cup of tea, respond to a text message, or perform a quick yoga stretch to prevent couch-induced muscle cramps.

"Become a Cricket Terminology Expert": Cricket has its own unique terminology that can leave newcomers scratching their heads. Brush up on terms like "wicket," "lbw," and "googly" to impress your fellow viewers with your cricket knowledge. Just be prepared to explain the intricacies to anyone who asks.

"Embrace the Joy of Commentator Banter": Commentators are an integral part of the cricket-watching experience. Embrace their banter, catchphrases, and humorous anecdotes. They add a layer of entertainment and insight that enhances your understanding of the game – or at least makes you chuckle.

"Master the Art of Emotional Roller Coaster Rides": Cricket is known for its nail-biting moments and sudden turnarounds. Prepare yourself for emotional roller coaster rides that can range from euphoria to despair within seconds. Remember to hold on tight and ride the waves of emotions with fellow fans.

"Don't Be Afraid to Embrace Superstitions": Cricket fans are notorious for their superstitions. If wearing your lucky socks or sitting in a particular spot brings your team good fortune, don't hesitate to follow these rituals. Just be prepared for some friendly teasing from your non-superstitious friends.

"Join the Twitterati": Twitter is the virtual stadium of cricket fans. Join the conversation by live-tweeting the match, using witty hashtags, and engaging in banter with fellow cricket enthusiasts. Just remember to keep your tweets concise and avoid spelling errors when excitement takes over.

"Appreciate the Slow Motion Replay": One of the joys of watching cricket on TV is the slow-motion replay. Take a moment to appreciate the elegance of a cover drive or the precision of a fast bowler's action. You might even pick up a few tips to improve your own cricket skills (or at least look good trying).

"Share the Experience": Watching cricket is more fun when shared with friends and family. Invite them over, create a festive atmosphere, and engage in friendly banter throughout the match. Remember, cricket is not just about the game; it's about creating lasting memories with loved ones.

So, grab your remote, gather your snacks, and get ready for a thrilling cricket-watching experience on TV. Remember, it's not just about the game itself – it's about the laughter, the camaraderie, and the shared passion for the sport. Enjoy the match, and may your team emerge victorious!

Attending live cricket events

Attending a live cricket event is an exhilarating experience that every cricket fan should have on their bucket list. The atmosphere, the energy, and the collective excitement of the crowd create an unforgettable ambiance. To ensure you make the most of your live cricket experience, here are some humorous yet practical tips:

"Get Your Tickets Early, or Risk Being Stumped": The demand for cricket tickets can be as high as an umpire's finger. Make sure you secure your tickets well in advance to avoid disappointment. Don't be caught out by leaving it too late and missing out on the chance to witness the action live.

"Dress to Impress, or At Least to Stay Comfortable": When it comes to dressing for a live cricket event, you have two options: blend in with team colors or go all out with outrageous costumes and face paint. Either way, make sure you wear comfortable shoes because you never know when you might need to sprint to catch that elusive six.

"Don't Forget Your Sunscreen, Unless You Want to Look Like a Red Cherry": Cricket matches can last for hours, and the sun can be unforgiving. Protect yourself from becoming a sunburnt spectacle by slathering on sunscreen and wearing a hat. You don't want to be mistaken for a lobster in the crowd.

"Channel Your Inner Foodie, But Beware the Sticker Shock": Live cricket events offer a variety of mouthwatering food options. From classic stadium snacks like hot dogs and burgers to international cuisines, there's something for everyone. Just be prepared for the hefty prices that can sometimes feel like a run-out decision gone wrong.

"Timing is Everything: Arrive Early to Secure the Best Seats": If you want the best view of the match, arrive early and claim your spot. Whether it's in the stands or on the grassy outfield, a good vantage point can make all the difference. Plus, arriving early gives you the opportunity to soak up the pre-match atmosphere and engage in some friendly banter with fellow fans.

"Be a Chanting Champ, but Remember to Pace Yourself": The atmosphere at live cricket events is electric, with chants and cheers filling the air. Join in the fun by learning the team chants and becoming a chanting champ. Just remember to pace yourself, as there's a long game ahead, and you don't want to lose your voice by the first innings.

"Bring Your Cricket Knowledge, but Be Open to Learning": A live cricket event is a great opportunity to showcase your cricket knowledge. But also be open to learning from other fans around you. You might pick up some interesting trivia or gain a new perspective on the game.

"Capture the Magic, but Don't Miss the Moment": It's tempting to capture every moment on your smartphone, but don't get so caught up in capturing the perfect selfie that you miss the actual live action. Take a few snaps to document the experience, but make sure to put the phone down and immerse yourself in the excitement.

"Embrace the Rain Delay Drama": In cricket, rain delays are as unpredictable as an umpire's decision. Be prepared for sudden interruptions due to rain and use the time to bond with fellow fans, explore the food stalls, or engage in a lively debate about cricket's greatest players.

"Remember, It's More Than a Game": Attending a live cricket event is about more than just watching a match. It's about joining a community of passionate fans, sharing in the excitement, and creating memories that last a lifetime. Soak up the atmosphere, cheer on your team, and revel in the joy of being part of the cricketing fraternity.

So, grab your tickets, don your team colors, and get ready for an unforgettable live cricket experience. Enjoy the roar of the crowd, the thrill of the game, and the camaraderie that comes with being part of a global cricketing family. And who knows, you might even catch a ball in the crowd or feature in a viral fan video. So, go forth and embrace the magic of live cricket!

Cricket fan culture and traditions

Cricket fan culture is as diverse and spirited as the game itself. From the iconic chants to the outrageous costumes, cricket fans bring an unparalleled level of enthusiasm and passion to the sport. Here, we delve into the colorful world of cricket fan culture and traditions with a touch of humor:

"Chants and Cheers: More Than Just Words": Cricket fans are known for their catchy and often amusing chants and cheers. From the classic "Ole, Ole, Ole" to the rhythmic "Barmy Army," these chants unite fans and create an electric atmosphere in the stadium. Join in the chorus, learn the lyrics, and let your voice be heard. Just remember to keep it PG and family-friendly!

"Dress to Impress, or at Least to Stand Out": When it comes to cricket fan fashion, anything goes. From wearing team jerseys to donning outrageous costumes, fans let their creativity shine. Want to dress as a banana or a superhero? Go for it! Just make sure your outfit doesn't obstruct the view of the person sitting behind you, or you might face a serious LBW (Limited Visibility Woe).

"The Art of the Banner: Creativity on Display": Banners and placards are a common sight in cricket stadiums. Fans use these colorful creations to display their witty slogans, messages of support, and even some gentle ribbing of the opposition. If you're feeling artistic, grab a marker and design your own masterpiece. Just be prepared for the wind to have a mind of its own and turn your carefully crafted banner into a flag of surrender.

"Rain Delays: When Fans Make Their Own Entertainment": Cricket matches are not immune to rain delays, which can be both frustrating and amusing. When the rain starts pouring, fans often find creative ways to pass the time. From impromptu dance-offs to organizing their own cricket matches in the stands, fans show their resilience and ability to make the best of a soggy situation.

"Food and Drinks: Fueling the Cricket Spirit": No cricket match is complete without indulging in some delicious stadium food and beverages. From classic stadium snacks like hot dogs and nachos to local culinary delights, fans satisfy their cravings while cheering on their teams. Just be careful not to spill that ketchup on your favorite team jersey, or you might end up with a permanent reminder of your snacking mishap.

"Friendly Banter: The Art of the Verbal Sledge": Cricket fans love a good banter session with opposition supporters. It's all in good fun, with fans engaging in witty exchanges, humorous insults, and playful jabs. Just remember to keep it light-hearted and respectful. After all, it's a game, not a battle of wits (unless you're competing for the title of the Funniest Cricket Fan in the World).

"The Spirit of Camaraderie: Bonds Beyond Borders": Cricket has a unique way of bringing people from different backgrounds and cultures together. At a cricket match, you'll find fans from all walks of life, united by their love for the game. Strike up a conversation with your fellow fans, share stories, and revel in the camaraderie that transcends boundaries.

"Creating Memories: Snapshots of Joy": Cricket matches are the perfect backdrop for creating lasting memories. Capture the moment with your friends and family, take selfies with fellow fans, and share your experiences on social media. Just make sure you don't miss out on the action while searching for the perfect angle or dealing with a selfie stick malfunction.

"Traveling the World: From Stadium to Stadium": For die-hard cricket fans, following their favorite teams across the globe is a dream come true. From the historic Lords in England to the iconic Melbourne Cricket Ground in Australia, these fans embark on cricket pilgrimages, immersing themselves in different cultures and experiencing cricket in its various forms.

"Passing on the Legacy: Introducing the Next Generation": Cricket fan culture is not limited to one generation. Parents pass down their love for the game to their children, creating a multi-generational bond. Whether it's attending matches together, playing backyard cricket, or watching games on TV, cricket becomes a shared passion that strengthens family ties.

Cricket fan culture is a vibrant and exciting world that enhances the enjoyment of the game. So, grab your team jersey, practice your chants, and immerse yourself in the unique experience of being a cricket fan. After all, it's not just about the game, but the camaraderie, the traditions, and the memories that make it truly special.

Cricket and Culture

Cricket is more than just a sport; it's a cultural phenomenon that has deeply ingrained itself in the fabric of many societies. Let's explore the unique relationship between cricket and culture with a touch of humor:

"The Great Leveller: Cricket Bridges Social Divides": Cricket has the power to bring people from all walks of life together. Whether you're a CEO or a street vendor, when you're on the cricket field, all that matters is your skill with the bat or ball. So, next time you find yourself batting alongside a celebrity, remember that in cricket, everyone is equal... well, at least until the ball hits the stumps.

"Cricket Fever: The Truest Sign of a Nation's Passion": In many cricket-loving nations, the game is not just a sport; it's a way of life. The passion for cricket runs deep, and you'll find the entire nation glued to their screens during important matches. Don't be surprised if you see streets empty and shops closed as the country unites in front of televisions, cheering on their team. It's like witnessing a synchronized national nap time, except with a lot more excitement.

"Cricket and Colonial Legacy: A Love Story with a Twist": Cricket's history is intertwined with colonialism, as the sport was introduced by the British Empire. But what's fascinating is how former colonies have embraced cricket as their own. It's like taking a gift from your ex and turning it into something you love and cherish. So, while the colonial roots remain, the game has evolved to reflect the diverse cultures and identities of cricket-playing nations.

"Cricket as Cultural Identity: More Than Just a Game": For many nations, cricket is not just a sport; it's a representation of their cultural identity. The playing styles, celebrations, and even the culinary traditions associated with cricket reflect the unique heritage of each country. So, the next time you see a player performing a victory dance, remember that it's not just a celebration; it's a showcase of their cultural flair.

"Cricket and Music: The Perfect Duet": Cricket and music go hand in hand. Whether it's the catchy anthems played during matches or the songs dedicated to cricket heroes, music adds an extra dimension to the cricketing experience. It's like having a personal soundtrack playing in the background as you witness breathtaking catches and daring sixes. Just be careful not to start singing along too loudly in the stands.

"Cricket and Fashion: Style on and off the Field": Cricket has also made its mark on the fashion world. From stylish team jerseys to fashionable accessories, cricket has influenced the way fans dress and express their support. So, the next time you see someone rocking a cricket-inspired outfit, remember that they're not just fashion-forward; they're also paying homage to the sport they love.

"Cricket and Humor: A Match Made in Comedy Heaven": Cricket has inspired a wealth of humor and comedy. From witty commentary to hilarious anecdotes shared by players, the game brings out the lighter side of life. So, don't be surprised if you find yourself laughing out loud while watching a cricket match. Just make sure you're not holding a cup of hot tea when the jokes land.

Cricket and culture are inseparable, and the sport continues to shape and be shaped by the societies that embrace it. From the shared excitement during matches to the diverse expressions of fan support, cricket transcends boundaries and creates connections. So, next time you find yourself caught up in the cricketing frenzy, remember that you're not just witnessing a game; you're experiencing a cultural phenomenon that unites people and brings joy to millions around the world.

The role of cricket in different cultures

Cricket, known as the "gentleman's game," holds a special place in the hearts of people across various cultures. Let's explore how cricket has become an integral part of different societies, with a sprinkle of humor:

"Cricket in India: More Than a Sport, It's a Religion": In India, cricket is nothing short of a religion. The passion and frenzy that surround the game are unparalleled. People worship their cricket idols, and matches can evoke a range of emotions from sheer elation to heartbreak. It's like witnessing a battle between cricket demigods and their devoted followers.

"Cricket Down Under: An Aussie Obsession and the Ashes Rivalry": In Australia, cricket is more than just a game; it's an obsession. The rivalry with England in the Ashes series is legendary, with witty banter and good-natured sledging adding spice to the competition. It's like a battle for bragging rights that stretches beyond the cricket field and into the hearts of fans.

"Caribbean Cricket: A Carnival of Calypso and Sixes": In the Caribbean, cricket is a celebration of rhythm and flair. The energetic Calypso music, vibrant costumes, and power-hitting batsmen make the matches a true spectacle. It's like a Caribbean carnival where the players dance to the rhythm of the game and send the ball soaring into the stands.

"Cricket in England: Tradition, Tea, and the Spirit of Fair Play": In England, cricket is synonymous with tradition and elegance. The sound of leather on willow, players sipping tea during breaks, and the unwavering spirit of fair play are all part of the English cricketing experience. It's like stepping into a time machine that takes you back to a bygone era of cricketing sophistication.

"Cricket in Pakistan: A Passionate Nation's Love Affair": In Pakistan, cricket unites the nation and serves as a source of pride and joy. The raw talent of Pakistani players, their unpredictable performances, and the roaring crowds in stadiums create an electrifying atmosphere. It's like witnessing a rollercoaster ride of emotions, where anything can happen, and the unexpected becomes the norm.

"Cricket in South Africa: A Symbol of Unity and Triumph Over Apartheid": In South Africa, cricket played a significant role in uniting the nation and breaking the chains of apartheid. The triumphs of the Proteas on the cricket field symbolize the resilience and determination of the South African people. It's like a beacon of hope that shows how sport can bring about social change.

"Cricket in New Zealand: Where Sportsmanship and Beauty Collide": In New Zealand, cricket is characterized by its sportsmanship, fair play, and stunning natural backdrops. The Kiwi players' humility and respect for the game are refreshing, and the scenic cricket grounds add a touch of beauty to every match. It's like watching cricket in paradise, where even the seagulls seem to cheer along.

Cricket's role in different cultures goes beyond just a sport. It becomes a reflection of the values, traditions, and aspirations of the people. Whether it's the religious fervor in India, the Aussie obsession in Australia, or the unity in South Africa, cricket serves as a platform for communities to come together, celebrate, and compete.

So, the next time you witness the excitement and fervor surrounding cricket in various cultures, remember that it's not just a game being played; it's a display of the unique spirit, identity, and collective joy of a nation.

Famous cricket players and teams

Cricket has witnessed the rise of numerous legendary players and iconic teams throughout its history. Let's take a lighthearted journey through some of the most famous cricket players and teams:

"Sir Don Bradman: The Invincible Wall of Cricket": Don Bradman, known as "The Don," was a cricketing phenomenon. His batting average of 994 remains unparalleled, earning him the nickname "The Invincible Wall." Rumor has it that bowlers would often check if their deliveries were in line with the laws of physics when facing him.

"Sachin Tendulkar: The Master Blaster": Sachin Tendulkar, or "The Little Master," is an Indian cricket icon. With a career spanning over two decades, he amassed a staggering number of runs and records. It is said that when he walked onto the pitch, the opposing team's captain would consider summoning divine intervention.

"Muralitharan: The Spinning Wizard": Muttiah Muralitharan, a Sri Lankan spin wizard, holds the record for the most wickets in Test cricket. His unorthodox bowling action, combined with his remarkable accuracy, made him a nightmare for batsmen. It's rumored that batsmen would take extra care in gripping their bats to ensure they didn't slip out of their hands against his spin.

"The West Indies: Calypso Kings of Cricket": The West Indies cricket team, known as the "Calypso Kings," dominated the game for years. With a formidable lineup of fast bowlers and explosive batsmen, they struck fear into the hearts of their opponents. It's said that their bouncers had more rhythm than a Caribbean steel band.

"The Australian Team: Baggy Green Champions": The Australian cricket team, adorned in their famous baggy green caps, has been a force to reckon with for decades. With players like Steve Waugh, Ricky Ponting, and Shane Warne, they formed a formidable lineup that left their opponents feeling as if they were facing a kangaroo stampede.

"The Pakistani Team: Unpredictability at its Finest": The Pakistani cricket team has earned a reputation for being both thrilling and unpredictable. Their flair for dramatic comebacks and unexpected victories keeps fans on the edge of their seats. It's like watching a high-stakes magic show where the trick is to never reveal their next move.

"The England Team: Cricket's Gentlemen": The England cricket team, known for their traditional white attire, embodies the spirit of the game. With players like Sir Ian Botham, Andrew Flintoff, and James Anderson, they have showcased the essence of cricketing elegance. It's as if they stepped straight out of a Jane Austen novel and onto the cricket pitch.

These famous players and teams have left an indelible mark on the history of cricket. Their talent, charisma, and remarkable achievements have entertained and inspired fans around the world. From Bradman's unbeatable records to Tendulkar's mastery and the collective prowess of teams like the West Indies and Australia, cricket has witnessed some unforgettable moments.

So, the next time you watch a cricket match or engage in a debate about the greatest players and teams, remember the legends who have graced the sport. They have not only left a lasting impact on the game but also provided us with countless moments of joy, excitement, and a fair share of humorous anecdotes.

Cricket controversies and scandals

Cricket, like any other sport, has had its fair share of controversies and scandals that have sparked debates and raised eyebrows among fans. While these incidents may have caused uproar at the time, they have also added a touch of drama and intrigue to the game. Let's take a light-hearted look at some of the most notable controversies and scandals in cricket:

"The Underarm Delivery Debacle": In 1981, during a match between Australia and New Zealand, the Australian captain Greg Chappell instructed his brother Trevor to bowl the final ball underarm, effectively preventing the New Zealand batsman from hitting a six to tie the match. The incident caused outrage and led to a change in the rules to ban underarm bowling. From then on, cricketers were only allowed to bowl overarm, avoiding the awkwardness of crawling on the ground like a crab.

"The Ball-Tampering Saga": In 2018, the Australian cricket team found themselves embroiled in a ball-tampering scandal during a Test match against South Africa. Cameron Bancroft was caught on camera attempting to alter the condition of the ball using sandpaper. The incident sparked worldwide debate and resulted in suspensions for the players involved. It also led to an increase in the sales of sandpaper in hardware stores, with curious customers claiming it was for "cricket practice."

"The Monkeygate Scandal": During the 2007-2008 Test series between Australia and India, a heated exchange between Indian player Harbhajan Singh and Australian all-rounder Andrew Symonds led to allegations of racial abuse. The incident, known as the "Monkeygate scandal," created a storm of controversy, with both teams fiercely defending their players. As a precaution, spectators were advised against throwing bananas onto the field during matches, even if they were hungry.

"The Match-Fixing Menace": Cricket has also had its share of match-fixing scandals, where players and officials conspired to manipulate the outcome of matches for personal gain. The most notable case involved prominent Pakistani cricketers, who were found guilty of spot-fixing during a Test match against England in 201 In response, cricket fans everywhere took up a new hobby called "spot-inspecting" where they scrutinized every suspicious movement on the field, from dropped catches to grass blades bending mysteriously.

"The DRS Drama": The Decision Review System (DRS) was introduced to eliminate umpiring errors, but it has also been the subject of controversy. Many instances have seen teams using their review calls in a strategic manner, hoping to overturn decisions in their favor. This has led to humorous moments where players have made "hopeful" review signals, resembling a fisherman casting a line or a magician conjuring a rabbit out of a hat.

While controversies and scandals can cast a shadow on the game, they also provide an opportunity for cricket to reflect, learn, and evolve. They remind us that cricket, like life itself, is not always a straight drive down the ground but a journey filled with twists, turns, and occasional googlies.

As fans, we can't help but discuss these controversies with fervor, speculating on the truth behind the headlines and concocting our own imaginative theories. After all, cricket without a few juicy controversies would be like a match without a six: entertaining, but missing that extra spark of excitement.

So, as we enjoy the game of cricket, let's appreciate both the fair play and the occasional controversies, because they all contribute to the rich tapestry of this wonderful sport. And who knows, the next controversy might just be lurking around the corner, ready to add another chapter to the ever-evolving history of cricket.

Cricket and Community

Cricket is not just a sport; it has the unique ability to bring communities together, creating a bond that transcends boundaries and unites people from different backgrounds. The spirit of cricket extends beyond the boundaries of the field and reaches deep into the heart of the community. Let's explore how cricket and community go hand in hand, with a touch of humor:

"The Local Cricket Club": Every community has its own local cricket club, where enthusiasts gather to play, cheer, and enjoy the game. These clubs serve as a hub for cricket lovers, providing a platform for players of all ages and skill levels to come together. They also act as a social gathering spot, where friendships are forged, and stories are shared over cups of tea and biscuits (or maybe a pint and some nachos if it's a modern club).

"Cricket Fundraisers": Community cricket matches are often organized as fundraisers for charitable causes. It's not uncommon to see a team of doctors challenging a team of lawyers, with each wicket and boundary contributing to a worthy cause. These matches not only raise funds but also bring the community together in support of a common goal. Plus, it's a chance for the lawyers to show their "argumentative" skills on the field and the doctors to showcase their "surgical precision" in their shots.

"Street Cricket": In many communities, especially in the streets of South Asia, cricket is played with improvised equipment and boundaries marked by bricks or trees. It's a lively and colorful spectacle, with children and adults alike showcasing their cricketing skills in the narrow lanes. Passing cars become obstacles, and windows sometimes bear the brunt of wayward shots. But hey, it's all in the spirit of neighborhood fun!

"Cricket Carnival": Community cricket tournaments are like mini-carnivals, complete with food stalls, music, and enthusiastic crowds. Families come together, setting up picnic spots on the sidelines and cheering for their favorite teams. The aroma of freshly cooked kebabs mixes with the excitement in the air, creating a festive atmosphere that is hard to resist. Just make sure not to drop your burger when the ball comes your way!

"Cricket Coaching Clinics": Many communities organize cricket coaching clinics to nurture young talent and instill a love for the game. These clinics provide aspiring cricketers with the opportunity to learn from experienced coaches and receive guidance from professionals. It's a chance for the young cricket stars of tomorrow to hone their skills, and who knows, maybe one day they'll be signing autographs instead of taking them!

Cricket has the power to unite people, break down barriers, and create a sense of belonging. It's not just about the game; it's about the laughter, camaraderie, and shared experiences that come with it. From local clubs to street matches, cricket brings communities together in a way that few other sports can.

So, whether you're a player, a spectator, or simply a cricket enthusiast, embrace the community spirit that cricket offers. Support your local team, engage in friendly banter with rival supporters, and cherish the memories created through this wonderful game.

After all, cricket is not just about the runs, wickets, and boundaries; it's about the joy, togetherness, and a little bit of humor that comes with being part of a cricketing community. So, grab your bat, put on your cricket hat, and join the vibrant and inclusive world of cricket where the community spirit thrives!

The impact of cricket on local communities

Cricket, a sport that is loved and cherished by millions around the world, has a significant impact on local communities. It goes beyond the boundaries of the field and leaves a lasting impression on the people and places it touches. Let's delve into the impact of cricket on local communities, with a sprinkle of humor:

"Community Bonding": Cricket acts as a catalyst for community bonding. Local cricket matches bring together people from different walks of life, creating a sense of unity and camaraderie. The match becomes a platform for individuals to connect, share stories, and cheer for their favorite teams. It's like a mini reunion where the only agenda is to enjoy the game and laugh at each other's enthusiastic shouts.

"Economic Boost": Cricket events, such as local tournaments or international matches held in a community, have a positive impact on the local economy. They attract spectators from near and far, leading to increased tourism, hotel bookings, and spending on food and beverages. The local vendors and businesses thrive during these events, and the streets are filled with the aroma of street food and the sound of cash registers ringing. It's a win-win situation for everyone involved, except maybe for the waistlines of the spectators indulging in the delicious treats.

"Social Integration": Cricket breaks down social barriers and promotes social integration within communities. It brings people of different backgrounds, ages, and social statuses together, fostering a sense of inclusivity and belonging. The cricket field becomes a melting pot where diversity is celebrated, and differences are set aside in the pursuit of the shared passion for the game. It's a beautiful sight to see a retired professor high-fiving a street vendor after a brilliant boundary.

"Youth Development": Cricket plays a vital role in youth development. It provides an avenue for young talents to showcase their skills, learn valuable life lessons, and develop essential qualities such as teamwork, discipline, and perseverance. Local cricket clubs and coaching programs offer structured training and mentorship, empowering young individuals to excel both on and off the field. Who knows, the next cricketing sensation might emerge from a small community, leaving everyone astonished and the pigeons worried about their safety.

"Community Pride": Cricket instills a sense of pride in local communities. When a local team achieves success, it boosts the morale and pride of the entire community. The team becomes a source of inspiration for aspiring cricketers and a symbol of community identity. The local streets are adorned with flags, banners, and painted faces, and everyone celebrates the success as if they had personally hit that winning six. It's a moment of collective joy and celebration that brings everyone together.

Cricket has the power to transcend boundaries and make a profound impact on local communities. It fosters a sense of belonging, promotes social cohesion, and drives economic growth. The game brings people together, creates memories, and leaves a lasting legacy within the hearts of the community.

So, let's embrace the impact of cricket on local communities, enjoy the game with friends and neighbors, and let the sound of laughter and cheers echo through the streets. Because, in the end, it's not just about the runs, wickets, or trophies; it's about the connections, the friendships, and the shared love for the game that make cricket a truly remarkable sport that brings communities together with a sprinkle of humor along the way.

Building cricket clubs and teams

Building cricket clubs and teams is an exciting endeavor that requires dedication, organization, and a dash of humor. Let's explore the process of creating and nurturing cricket clubs and teams, blending the informative with a sprinkle of humor:

"Gather the Enthusiasts": The first step in building a cricket club or team is to gather a group of enthusiastic individuals who share a love for the game. Spread the word in the community, post funny cricket memes on social media, and watch as like-minded cricket aficionados come together like ants to a picnic. Remember, a team that laughs together, stays together.

"Find a Home Ground": Every cricket club needs a home ground where the magic happens. Look for a suitable cricket pitch or convert a vacant field into a cricketing paradise. It may involve a few discussions with local authorities, navigating the bureaucracy with witty cricket analogies, and, of course, making sure the ground has a prime spot for the post-match tea and banter.

"Equip Your Team": No cricket team is complete without proper equipment. Ensure you have enough cricket bats, balls, stumps, and protective gear for all players. You don't want your players chasing after a tennis ball and using milk crates as makeshift wickets. It's all fun and games until someone bowls a full toss at the wicketkeeper's shin.

"Develop a Training Program": To build a successful team, you need to develop a training program that focuses on skill development and teamwork. Conduct regular practice sessions, drills, and net sessions. Don't forget to incorporate some unconventional drills, like catching cricket balls while wearing oven mitts or batting blindfolded (well, maybe not blindfolded). It's all about keeping things light-hearted and entertaining.

"Spread the Cricket Fever": Promote your cricket club or team within the community to attract more players and supporters. Organize cricket clinics for youngsters, host inter-club matches, or even organize a cricket-themed flash mob (because who doesn't love a spontaneous synchronized dance routine in cricket attire?). The key is to make cricket the talk of the town, leaving everyone wondering how a sport involving grass and a bat can create such excitement.

"Embrace Team Spirit": Building a strong team involves fostering a sense of camaraderie and team spirit. Organize team-building activities, like cricket-themed scavenger hunts or cricket trivia nights. Encourage team members to support each other, celebrate victories together, and console each other after an unfortunate run-out (hey, it happens to the best of us).

"Compete and Have Fun": Once your team is ready, it's time to enter local cricket leagues or tournaments. Remember, while winning is important, it's equally important to have fun and enjoy the game. Keep the spirit of cricket alive by playing in the true spirit of sportsmanship, and don't forget to exchange a friendly smile with the opponent even if they just hit a six off your best delivery.

Building cricket clubs and teams is a journey that brings people together, fosters lifelong friendships, and creates memories that last a lifetime. So, gather your cricket-loving friends, put on your cricket whites (or colorful jerseys), and embark on this adventure with a blend of determination and humor. Because in the end, it's not just about the game; it's about the joy, laughter, and the thrill of hitting a well-timed cover drive while maintaining your balance (or at least trying to).

So, go ahead, build your cricket club or team, and let the sound of leather hitting willow resonate through the community, bringing smiles and unforgettable moments. And remember, in the game of cricket, the real victory lies in the bonds forged, the friendships made, and the shared laughter that echoes across the cricket field.

Promoting cricket among youth

Promoting cricket among youth is not just about introducing them to a sport; it's about instilling a lifelong passion, creating a new generation of cricket enthusiasts, and, of course, having some fun along the way. Let's dive into the world of youth cricket promotion with a touch of humor:

"Cricket: The Coolest Sport You've Never Heard Of": To get the attention of young minds, you need to highlight the coolness factor of cricket. Start by explaining that cricket is a sport that involves funny-shaped bats, outfits that resemble pajamas, and a tea break during the game (because who doesn't love a good cuppa?). Emphasize that cricket is more than a sport; it's a chance to be part of a quirky and entertaining tradition.

"Make Cricket Accessible": To promote cricket among youth, it's essential to make the sport accessible. Provide equipment and facilities in schools and local communities, ensuring that cricket is within reach for everyone. And remember, it's not just about the cricket pitch; it's about creating an atmosphere where young players can unleash their inner cricket superstar and chase their dreams.

"Introduce T20 Cricket: The Cricket Express": T20 cricket has revolutionized the game, bringing fast-paced action, big hits, and nail-biting finishes. Introduce young players to the excitement of T20 cricket, explaining that it's like cricket on steroids (not literally, of course!). Emphasize the thrill of hitting sixes and taking wickets in a shorter time, keeping young minds engaged and captivated.

"Cricket Superheroes: From Sachin to Kohli": Showcase the iconic cricket stars who have captured the world's imagination. Share stories of cricket legends like Sachin Tendulkar, Brian Lara, and Virat Kohli, emphasizing their remarkable skills, records, and the moments that make cricket history. Let the youth know that cricket can turn them into heroes too (well, at least in their backyard matches).

"Create Youth Cricket Leagues": Establishing youth cricket leagues can provide a platform for young players to showcase their talents and compete with their peers. Encourage friendly competition, sportsmanship, and fair play. And don't forget to sprinkle some humor into the league matches with funny team names, hilarious nicknames, and memorable victory celebrations.

"Cricket Clinics and Camps: Where Magic Happens": Organize cricket clinics and camps where experienced coaches share their knowledge and passion for the game. Make the sessions interactive, incorporating fun drills, mini-games, and challenges. And who knows, you might discover the next cricket prodigy who can bat like a boss or bowl like a magician.

"Cricket Mania: Social Media Style": Leverage the power of social media to create a buzz around cricket. Share funny cricket memes, engaging videos, and captivating cricket trivia. Encourage young players to share their cricketing adventures, catch their most epic catches on camera, and celebrate their victories with hilarious victory dances. Let cricket mania take over the internet!

Promoting cricket among youth is all about capturing their imagination, making the sport relatable, and creating an environment where they can enjoy and excel. Remember, humor is a powerful tool that can break down barriers, ignite passion, and make the journey of promoting cricket a memorable one.

So, unleash your inner cricket ambassador, share the joy of cricket with the youth, and watch as they become cricket-crazy, wielding bats like superheroes and celebrating wickets with infectious laughter. Because in the world of cricket, it's not just about the game; it's about the memories, friendships, and laughter that come along with it.

Getting Involved in Cricket

Cricket, a sport that has captured the hearts of millions around the world, offers a unique blend of excitement, camaraderie, and a touch of British eccentricity. If you're itching to get involved in the cricketing world, here's a guide on how to join the cricketing frenzy, sprinkled with a pinch of humor:

"Finding Your Inner Cricket Fanatic": First things first, embrace your inner cricket fanatic. Be prepared to lose track of time while engrossed in matches, passionately debate LBW decisions with friends, and develop an insatiable appetite for cricket trivia. You'll soon find yourself immersed in the wonderful world of cricket.

"Choose Your Role: Player or Spectator?": Cricket offers opportunities for both active participation and enthusiastic spectating. If you're eager to get on the field, find a local cricket club and join their ranks. Whether you're a batting maestro, a spin wizard, or a lightning-fast fielder, there's a role for everyone. If spectating is more your style, grab your popcorn, choose a favorite team, and settle in for an entertaining cricket match from the comfort of your couch.

"Mastering the Art of Bat and Ball": If you're keen on becoming a player, it's time to master the art of bat and ball. Attend coaching sessions, hone your batting technique, and learn the intricacies of bowling. And remember, practice makes perfect, so be prepared to spend countless hours in the nets, perfecting your shots and delivery. But don't forget to laugh at your own quirky attempts along the way.

"Gear Up, Cricket-Style": As a player, you'll need the right gear to protect yourself and unleash your cricketing prowess. Invest in a quality bat that feels like an extension of your arm, and don't forget the protective gear: helmet, pads, gloves, and an abdominal guard (yes, it's called a box!). You'll be a walking fortress ready to face any cricket challenge.

"Cricket Fashion: Channel Your Inner Fashionista": Cricket has its own unique fashion sense, blending tradition with a touch of quirkiness. Embrace the cricketing fashionista within you by donning stylish cricket whites or vibrant team jerseys. And of course, don't forget the iconic floppy hat or the cool sunglasses to complete your cricketing ensemble.

"Befriend the Cricket Rulebook": Cricket is a sport with an elaborate rulebook that can sometimes be as confusing as advanced calculus. But fear not, embrace the rulebook as your cricketing bible. Familiarize yourself with the LBW rule, the intricacies of field placements, and the DRS (Decision Review System). It's all part of the cricketing journey, and a few humorous rule misinterpretations along the way are to be expected.

"Cheer, Chant, and Celebrate": Whether you're on the field or in the stands, cricket is all about expressing your emotions. Cheer on your teammates, join in with the crowd chants, and celebrate every wicket or boundary like it's the greatest achievement in cricket history. Let your enthusiasm shine and embrace the infectious energy of cricket.

Getting involved in cricket is a ticket to a world of excitement, camaraderie, and unforgettable moments. So, whether you're donning the cricket whites, perfecting your cricket knowledge, or immersing yourself in the cricketing atmosphere, remember to enjoy the journey and let humor be your trusty companion along the way.

Cricket offers a unique blend of sporting excellence and lighthearted entertainment, where you can witness breathtaking performances, engage in lively banter, and forge lifelong friendships. So, jump into the world of cricket, embrace the spirit of the game, and get ready for an adventure filled with laughter, passion, and memorable cricketing moments.

Joining a local cricket team or club

Are you ready to hit the cricketing pitch and become a part of the vibrant cricketing community? Joining a local cricket team or club is a fantastic way to immerse yourself in the sport, forge new friendships, and showcase your cricketing skills. Let's dive into the world of joining a cricket team, sprinkled with a touch of humor along the way:

"Scouting for the Perfect Team": Start your cricketing journey by scouting for the perfect team or club in your local area. Check out community notice boards, social media groups, or ask fellow cricket enthusiasts for recommendations. Look for a team that aligns with your skill level, aspirations, and perhaps a team with a sense of humor to match yours.

"Dusting Off Your Cricketing Skills": Whether you're a seasoned cricketer or new to the sport, it's time to dust off your cricketing skills. Attend practice sessions, net sessions, and training camps to brush up on your batting, bowling, and fielding techniques. Don't be afraid to make a few comical blunders along the way. After all, laughter is the best cure for cricketing jitters.

"The Trials and Tribulations of Team Selection": Ah, the dreaded team selection process. Brace yourself for the trials and tribulations of trying to impress the selectors. It's a nerve-wracking experience, but remember that even the greatest cricketing legends faced rejection at some point. Keep a light-hearted attitude, take it as a learning experience, and don't forget to showcase your unique personality on and off the field.

"Befriending Your Teammates": Joining a cricket team is not just about playing the sport; it's also about forging lifelong friendships. Embrace the camaraderie with your teammates and make an effort to befriend them. After all, you'll be spending hours together, sharing laughter, victories, and the occasional defeat. Crack a few jokes, engage in friendly banter, and cherish the bond that cricket brings.

"The Curious World of Cricket Lingo": Cricket has its own peculiar language, filled with confusing terms and baffling slang. Prepare yourself for an initiation into the curious world of cricket lingo. From googlies to yorkers, dibbly-dobblies to dilscoops, you'll encounter a plethora of amusing terms. Don't worry if you feel lost at first; it's all part of the cricketing adventure.

"Match Day Mania": Match days are the heart and soul of cricketing life. Get ready for the match day mania, where you'll experience a rollercoaster of emotions, from nervous anticipation to thrilling moments of success. Don your team's colors, practice your victory dance, and get ready to immerse yourself in the electrifying atmosphere of competitive cricket.

"Celebrating Victories and Learning from Defeats": In cricket, there will be moments of triumph and moments of defeat. Celebrate the victories with gusto and learn from the defeats with grace. Remember, it's not just about winning but also about the friendships forged and the memories created along the way. Keep a light-hearted spirit, laugh off the occasional misfield or missed catch, and relish the journey of cricketing camaraderie.

Joining a local cricket team or club opens up a world of opportunities, laughter, and unforgettable experiences. So, gather your cricketing gear, embrace the spirit of teamwork, and get ready for a cricketing adventure filled with humor, camaraderie, and thrilling moments on and off the field.

Participating in cricket leagues and events

Cricket leagues and events provide an exciting platform for cricket enthusiasts to showcase their skills, engage in spirited competition, and bask in the glory of the game. Whether you're a seasoned player or a cricket enthusiast eager to participate, joining cricket leagues and events promises a thrilling experience. Let's dive into the world of cricketing competitions, sprinkled with a touch of humor:

"Finding the Right League": With numerous cricket leagues and events happening around, finding the right one for you can be as perplexing as deciphering a googly. Consider factors such as format, skill level, and location when selecting a league. Remember, you want to strike a balance between competitive cricket and a fun-filled environment. Think of it as finding the perfect cricketing pitch to showcase your talent.

"Team Formation Woes": Participating in a cricket league means teaming up with fellow cricket enthusiasts, which can lead to some amusing team formation woes. From the meticulous selection of captains to the strategizing of draft picks, it's a battle of cricketing minds. Embrace the unpredictability, cross your fingers for a skilled team, and hope you don't end up with a team full of bowlers who think they're batsmen.

"The Art of Uniform Selection": In cricket leagues, teams often don distinctive uniforms that make them stand out on the field. From colorful jerseys to flamboyant caps, the art of uniform selection can turn into a fashion contest. Just remember, it's not about how fashionable your uniform is but how well you perform in it. Besides, a bright and eye-catching uniform might distract your opponents, giving you a winning edge.

"The Thrill of Match Days": Match days in cricket leagues are the epitome of excitement. The thumping heartbeat, the pre-match rituals, and the feeling of stepping onto the field – it's a cocktail of nerves and exhilaration. Celebrate the thrill of match days, savor the banter with opponents, and be ready for some epic on-field showdowns. After all, cricket is not just about winning; it's about the joy of the game.

"Unleashing Your Signature Moves": Cricket leagues provide the perfect platform to unleash your signature cricketing moves. Whether it's a blistering cover drive or a deceptive slower ball, bring out your A-game and dazzle the spectators with your skills. And don't forget to add a touch of showmanship; a well-executed celebration or a witty one-liner can add to the amusement.

"Navigating the Politics": Like any competitive event, cricket leagues are not immune to the occasional politics and drama. Navigating through team rivalries, disputes over umpiring decisions, and post-match debates can be as challenging as reading a spinner's variations. Keep your sense of humor intact, rise above the politics, and remember that cricket is ultimately a game that brings people together.

Participating in cricket leagues and events offers a chance to be a part of the cricketing extravaganza, showcasing your talent, and creating lasting memories. So, grab your cricket gear, tighten your shoelaces, and get ready to unleash your cricketing prowess on the field. Let the cricketing battles, laughter, and camaraderie begin in the realm of cricket leagues and events.

Opportunities for cricket volunteerism and leadership

Cricket isn't just about playing the game; it also presents a myriad of opportunities for volunteerism and leadership. Whether you're a cricket enthusiast looking to give back to the community or a passionate individual seeking to enhance your leadership skills, cricket offers a platform for both. Let's explore the exciting world of cricket volunteerism and leadership with a dash of humor:

"Scoring Big with Scorekeeping": Scorekeeping is an essential aspect of cricket, and volunteering as a scorer can be a rewarding experience. It requires sharp focus, attention to detail, and the ability to decipher the complexities of cricket scoring. Plus, you'll get a front-row seat to witness the ebb and flow of the game, and maybe even showcase your witty banter with the players.

"Coaching: Shaping Future Legends": If you have a passion for cricket and enjoy sharing your knowledge, consider volunteering as a cricket coach. It's your chance to shape the future cricketing stars and help them develop their skills. But be prepared for amusing moments when you realize that teaching youngsters how to hold a cricket bat can feel like teaching them how to ride a unicycle!

"Umpiring: The Art of Making Decisions": Umpiring is a critical role in cricket, ensuring fair play and upholding the rules. It's an opportunity to showcase your knowledge of the game, but be prepared for some humorous moments when players question your decisions, believing they have the best eyesight on the field.

"Ground Maintenance: The Unsung Heroes": Behind every successful cricket match, there's a team of dedicated individuals maintaining the ground. From mowing the grass to preparing the pitch, volunteering in ground maintenance is a chance to contribute to the game's infrastructure. Just be ready for the unexpected encounters with mischievous squirrels who think the pitch is their personal playground.

"Organizing Cricket Events: A Grand Affair": Cricket events require meticulous planning and organization. Volunteering in event management provides an opportunity to showcase your leadership skills. From coordinating teams and scheduling matches to managing logistics, it's a chance to shine as a leader. Just remember to keep your cool when the inevitable last-minute changes throw a googly your way.

"Community Outreach: Spreading Cricket Love": Cricket has the power to bring communities together. Volunteering in community outreach programs allows you to introduce the joy of cricket to individuals who may not have had the opportunity to play before. From organizing cricket clinics to creating inclusive cricket programs, it's a chance to share your passion for the game and witness the transformational impact it can have on lives.

Engaging in cricket volunteerism and leadership not only allows you to contribute to the cricketing ecosystem but also provides personal growth and fulfillment. So, grab your cricket gear, put on your leadership hat, and embrace the exciting opportunities that cricket offers. Just be prepared for moments when organizing a cricket event feels like herding cats!

In the realm of cricket volunteerism and leadership, the laughter, camaraderie, and sense of accomplishment are unparalleled. It's a chance to make a difference in the cricketing world while creating lasting memories and friendships. So, step up to the crease, take on the challenges, and let your passion for cricket shine through your volunteerism and leadership endeavors.

Conclusion

In conclusion, cricket is much more than a sport; it's a source of joy, excitement, and a platform for personal growth. From playing the game to getting involved in various aspects of cricket, there are endless opportunities to explore and immerse yourself in the cricketing world. Throughout this chapter, we've seen how cricket brings people together, fosters a sense of community, and offers avenues for personal development.

Whether you're a player, a fan, or someone who wants to contribute to the cricketing ecosystem, there's a role for everyone. From joining a local cricket team or club to participating in leagues and events, cricket provides a stage for individuals to showcase their skills, passion, and camaraderie.

We've explored the significance of coaching and mentoring, the excitement of playing in competitive leagues, the thrill of watching live cricket matches, and the fulfillment of volunteering and leadership roles. Cricket has the power to shape lives, instill discipline, and create lifelong friendships. And let's not forget the humorous moments that make the cricketing experience even more memorable.

Cricket's impact extends beyond the boundaries of the field. It influences cultures, strengthens communities, and promotes unity. It's a sport that transcends language, race, and nationality, captivating hearts across the globe.

As you delve into the world of cricket, remember to embrace the humor and light-heartedness that accompanies the game. Whether it's the banter between players, the comical situations during matches, or the friendly rivalry among fans, humor adds a delightful touch to the cricketing experience.

So, whether you're donning the cricket whites, analyzing the game from the comfort of your living room, or actively involved in cricket-related activities, remember that cricket is not just about the score, but about the connections and memories created along the way.

In the world of cricket, there's something for everyone. It's a sport that ignites passion, encourages teamwork, and celebrates individual brilliance. From the early morning dew on the field to the roar of the crowd, cricket is a symphony of emotions and experiences.

So, whether you're a seasoned player, a devoted fan, or someone curious to explore the world of cricket, seize the opportunity to be part of this magnificent game. Engage in the cricketing community, discover your role, and let the magic of cricket unfold in your life.

In the end, cricket is not just a game; it's a way of life. It teaches us resilience, sportsmanship, and the importance of teamwork. It brings people together, transcending boundaries and uniting diverse cultures under the common love for the sport.

So, grab your cricket bat, put on your cricket hat, and get ready to be a part of this wonderful cricketing journey. Remember, in cricket, the game is not just about winning or losing, but about the friendships, memories, and laughter that come along the way.

Embrace the spirit of cricket, let it weave its magic, and enjoy the wonderful journey that awaits you. The world of cricket is waiting, and it's time for you to make your mark.

Recap of key takeaways

As we reach the end of our cricketing adventure, let's take a moment to recap the key takeaways from our journey.

Firstly, cricket is more than just a game. It's a sport that brings people together, builds communities, and transcends cultural boundaries. Whether you're a player, a fan, or someone involved in cricket-related activities, there's a role for everyone in the cricketing world.

We've explored the different aspects of cricket, from playing the game to watching it on TV or attending live events. We've seen how cricket has its own unique set of rules, terminology, and strategies that make it both challenging and exciting.

We've witnessed the importance of teamwork and communication on the field. Cricket is a game where individual brilliance is celebrated, but success often hinges on the ability to work together as a cohesive unit. So, remember to value the contributions of your teammates and communicate effectively to achieve your collective goals.

We've also learned about the rich history of cricket, from its origins in England to its global expansion. Cricket has evolved over time, adapting to different formats and competitions. It has given rise to legendary players and iconic teams that have left a lasting impact on the sport.

Furthermore, we've explored the lighter side of cricket, with its moments of humor and banter. Whether it's the witty sledging between players or the funny incidents on the field, cricket has its fair share of comedic moments that add to the overall charm of the game.

Cricket is a sport that demands skill, dedication, and resilience. It teaches us important life lessons such as sportsmanship, discipline, and the value of perseverance. It's a sport that rewards hard work and talent, but also teaches us to embrace both success and failure with grace.

Moreover, cricket has a profound impact on local communities. It brings people together, fosters a sense of belonging, and creates opportunities for personal growth. From building cricket clubs and teams to promoting the sport among youth, cricket serves as a catalyst for positive change.

In summary, cricket is a sport that encapsulates the spirit of camaraderie, competition, and cultural diversity. It's a game that unites people from all walks of life, creating lifelong memories and forging lasting friendships.

As you continue your cricketing journey, whether as a player, a fan, or someone involved in the cricketing ecosystem, remember to cherish the experiences, embrace the challenges, and enjoy the moments of triumph and joy.

Cricket is not just a sport; it's a way of life. So, grab your cricket bat, don your cricket gear, and step onto the field with confidence and enthusiasm. And in those moments of doubt or setbacks, remember that cricket is meant to be enjoyed, to bring smiles to faces, and to create memories that last a lifetime.

So, let the spirit of cricket guide you, and may your cricketing adventure be filled with laughter, excitement, and a deep appreciation for the beautiful game.

Encouragement to play, watch, and enjoy cricket

Cricket, oh cricket! The sport that captivates hearts and ignites passion. If you haven't already dipped your toes into the world of cricket, it's time to grab your popcorn, don your cricket cap, and embark on an exhilarating journey of playing, watching, and enjoying this fantastic game.

Firstly, let's talk about playing cricket. Whether you're a seasoned player or a newbie, cricket offers an exciting opportunity to showcase your skills, have some fun, and maybe even unleash your hidden talent for hitting sixes. So, gather your friends, find an open space, and let the cricketing madness begin. Remember, even if you swing and miss, there's always the next ball to make it right.

But hey, don't worry if you don't fancy being a player. Watching cricket is a whole different ball game. Picture this: a sunny day, a packed stadium, and the roar of the crowd as the ball soars through the air. Watching cricket is like being part of a grand theater production, with moments of intense drama and unexpected plot twists. So, grab your remote, tune in to a match, and prepare to be entertained by the magic of the game.

Now, let's talk about enjoying cricket. Cricket is not just about the boundaries and wickets; it's about the overall experience. It's about the camaraderie among fans, the excitement of nail-biting finishes, and the joy of celebrating a well-played shot. So, immerse yourself in the game, soak up the atmosphere, and let the passion of cricket wash over you. Trust me, it's contagious!

One of the great things about cricket is that it brings people from different backgrounds and cultures together. It transcends borders and creates a global community of cricket enthusiasts. So, don't be surprised if you find yourself bonding with strangers over a shared love for the game. After all, cricket has a unique way of fostering friendships that can last a lifetime.

If you're feeling adventurous, why not explore cricket beyond the boundaries of your television screen? Attend a live match and witness the action unfold right before your eyes. Feel the energy in the stadium, cheer for your favorite team, and maybe even catch a flying cricket ball (but be sure to return it, the players might need it).

And let's not forget the moments of humor that cricket brings. From hilarious bloopers to witty on-field banter, cricket has its fair share of comic relief. Who can forget the infamous "ball tampering" incident or the amusing slip-ups that leave players red-faced? So, get ready to laugh, chuckle, and maybe even snort with amusement as you watch cricket's humorous side.

In conclusion, cricket is a sport that offers something for everyone. Whether you play, watch, or simply enjoy the camaraderie and excitement surrounding the game, cricket has a way of capturing hearts and leaving lasting memories. So, whether you're a die-hard fan or a curious newbie, it's time to embrace the world of cricket, immerse yourself in its magic, and let the game weave its spell on you.

Remember, cricket is not just a sport; it's a passion, a way of life. So, pick up that bat, cheer for your favorite team, and let the thrill of cricket fill your veins. And in those moments of doubt or defeat, remember that cricket is all about enjoying the journey, embracing the highs and lows, and celebrating the spirit of the game.

So, go ahead, dive into the world of cricket, and let the games begin!

Have Questions / Comments?

This book was designed to cover as much as possible but I know I have probably missed something, or some new amazing discovery that has just come out.

If you notice something missing or have a question that I failed to answer, please get in touch and let me know. If I can, I will email you an answer and also update the book so others can also benefit from it.

Thanks For Being Awesome :)

Submit Your Questions / Comments At:

https://go.xspurts.com/questions

1. https://xspurts.com/posts/questions

Get Another Book Free

We love writing and have produced a huge number of books.

For being one of our amazing readers, we would love to offer you another book we have created, 100% free.

To claim this limited time special offer, simply go to the site below and enter your name and email address.

You will then receive one of my great books, direct to your email account, 100% free!

https://go.xspurts.com/free-book-offer

---

1. https://xspurts.com/posts/free-book-offer

Also by Tavin D. Spicer

Understanding Cricket: A Guide to Playing, Watching, and Enjoying the Sport

Milton Keynes UK
Ingram Content Group UK Ltd.
UKHW021828031123
431730UK00012B/237

9 781776 847044